What to Do When You're Totally Screwed

What to Do When You're Totally Screwed

Simple Strategies for Bringing Your Life into Balance

Brian R. King, LCSW

iUniverse, Inc.
New York Lincoln Shanghai

What to Do When You're Totally Screwed
Simple Strategies for Bringing Your Life into Balance

All Rights Reserved © 2004 by Brian R. King

No part of this book may be reproduced or transmitted in any form or by any means, graphic, electronic, or mechanical, including photocopying, recording, taping, or by any information storage retrieval system, without the written permission of the publisher.

iUniverse, Inc.

For information address:
iUniverse, Inc.
2021 Pine Lake Road, Suite 100
Lincoln, NE 68512
www.iuniverse.com

ISBN: 0-595-33332-X (pbk)
ISBN: 0-595-66847-X (cloth)

Printed in the United States of America

This Book Is Dedicated to:

My Family and Friends
The Greatest Teammates a Guy Could Have

Thanks Is Owed to:

Katherine King (my wife)

Every time I set a goal for myself she continues to offer her unconditional support no matter what the risk. For no other reason than that she believes in me.

Zachary and Aidan King (my sons)

Two miracles in my life who are sources of endless joy as well as constant reminders of all of the new and wonderful things that each new day has to offer.

Marianne King (my mother and biggest fan)

There are no words to describe the value her support has brought to my life.

Jack Canfield (Co creator of *Chicken Soup for the Soul*)

He is without question the finest human being I've ever worked with and has taught me more about embracing my humanity than any 1,000 people I've met. I am also grateful to Jack for generously allowing me to share some of his teachings in this book.

Amanda Reid, MSW

Without her encouraging me to take my ideas out of my head and put them on paper, this book may have never been written.

Mary Beth Curran, Editor

For her guidance, professionalism and exceptional ability to help me craft my writing from simple words to a work of art.

Special Thanks to:

Virginia Zahaitis (my fourth-grade teacher) for always encouraging me to think positively when everything else around me was negative and making positivity so accessible in her presence.

Beverly Hajjar (my fifth-grade play director). She allowed me to be creative and encouraged as well as guided me to give nothing less than what I was capable of giving. She always made me feel that who I was was the best thing I could offer people.

Molly Gallagher (my sixth-grade teacher). She treated my early efforts at writing like works of art.

Barbara Clark (my seventh-grade counselor) for her unconditional support and guidance. She had an ability to help me feel powerful and confident when those around me were determined to take those feelings away.

Gail Aronoff (my 11th and 12th grade teacher). She always encouraged me to reach my highest potential of creativity, and when I reached it she encouraged me to go even higher. She continues to be a positive force as I continue on my path in life.

Don Zabelin (my 11th grade teacher) for his sense of humor and ability to be childlike and professional at the same time. He has a warm, optimistic spirit, which he saw and encouraged in me as well.

Ann Fagerland (my 12th grade teacher). She was the first English teacher I had that encouraged me to find my own voice in my writing. She supported my voice without judgment. It was during this time that I developed the ability to express myself with the written word, a skill that became indispensable when dealing with the most difficult time of my life.

Betty C. Andrews (my 12th grade teacher) She believed without a doubt that she would see me one day with my name in lights.

Of the thousands of people I've come across in my life, it was the people above that supported me consistently and unconditionally. They each appeared in my life at just the right time; some during a time when it seemed no one was on my side. It is often a single phrase, like Betty Andrews' prediction, that sends a person's thinking and life into a totally new and rewarding direction. The biggest lesson to be learned from them and others like them is that people will line up to discourage you, but when those that will support you show up, it makes all of the difference in the world.

Finding those special people in life is like panning for gold: You may spend years finding nothing more than dirt and rock, but one day you find the golden nugget you've been looking for that makes the entire journey worthwhile. When you find someone who believes in you, trust that belief unconditionally because what they see in you stems from the best parts of life: hopes, dreams, determination, good-will, unselfishness, compassion and honesty. Discouragement stems from those things that keep us from succeeding: fear, doubt, disbelief and anything else that compels us to seek safety in limited thinking instead of venturing out and taking the risks that lead to growth. It's the believers and risk takers who've made the world what it is. When they throw some of that belief your way, grab it. Hold on tight and ride it until it appears in your life the way it appears in your mind and in their hearts.

We all have dreams, but until we take action to realize them, we have no chance of living the life our heart and mind have showed us is right for us. So dream, dare, act and live fully.

Contents

Preface xiii
Introduction xv
Introducing, Your Life Team xix

Part I   *From Darkness to Light*

CHAPTER 1   My Story of Adversity 3
- *The Journey Begins* *3*
- *The Diagnosis* *7*
- *My Friends Receive the News* *9*
- *One Last Hurrah* *10*
- *Not So Fast* *11*
- *Round One* *13*
- *Hair Today, Gone Tomorrow* *17*
- *Round Two* *20*
- *I Reach Out for Support* *23*
- *The Downward Spiral* *24*

CHAPTER 2   From Suffering to Living 29
- *The First Step Toward Healing* *29*
- *The Hara Decision* *30*
- *Isolation* *32*
- *The Lesson of the Clock* *35*
- *The Bending of the Tree* *38*
- *The Lesson of the Leaf* *41*
- *A Child's Eyes* *42*

- *I Shall Be the Sun* 42
- *The Bird of Change* 43
- *F.E.A.R.* 44
- *Marking My Path* 46
- *Being Myself* 48
- *A Crack in the Soil* 50

Part II   A Cure for What Ails You

CHAPTER 3   The Responsibility Cure 55
- *Taking Responsibility and Taking Control* 56
- *Your Locus of Control* 58
- *Your Responsibilities* 60
- *Giving Your Mind Away* 63
- *The Search for Security* 64
- *Examine Your Expectations* 66
- *Setting and Working Your Goal* 71
- *Thinking Inside Out* 71
- *Partializing* 73
- *Assembling the Puzzle* 76

CHAPTER 4   Taking Life the Only Way It Comes 79
- *Moment to Moment* 79
- *The Moment Hand* 80
- *Minding the Breath, Minding the Hara* 81
- *External Body Scan* 84
- *Internal Body Scan* 86

CHAPTER 5   Immediacy 90
- *The Immediacy Skill* 91
  Rule #1: Don't lose track of your head 91
  Rule #2: Get off the time machine 92
- *Be Like Water* 94

CHAPTER 6   Living the Cure 95

- *The Black Hole of Victimhood* *95*
- *A Cure for Victim Thinking* *97*
- *Now You Know* *97*
- *The Attitude* *98*
- *The "No-You-Can't Rant"* *99*
- *The Credible Can't* *100*
- *Your Big "BUT"* *102*
- *Where to Go from "No"* *104*
- *Which One Are You?* *106*
- *What Is Your Life For?* *110*
- *The Three Attitudes for Achievement* *111*
- *The Failure Fallacy* *114*
- *Finding the Passion Within You: Coming up for Air* *114*
- *The Double H List* *117*

Chapter 7   Meaning Mastery *121*
- *The Truth Shall Set You Free! Or Will It?* *122*
- *The Meaning of Life* *123*
- *The Edge* *124*
- *Angel Training* *126*
- *Remembering Bill* *128*

Chapter 8   The ZAP *131*
- *Implementing the ZAP* *132*
- *Dealing with Negative People* *133*
- *Your Life Team Directory* *136*
- *Your Life Team Diary* *137*

Chapter 9   Becoming the Ultimate Starter *138*
- *Unlimited Hope* *140*
- *Being Right or Being Happy* *141*
- *The Right Thing to Do* *142*
- *Two Goals for Everyday Growth* *143*
- *Happy "Cure Day!"* *144*

- *Final Thoughts*... *146*

Bibliography 147
About the Author 149

Preface

First of all I want to thank you from the bottom of my heart for investing in this book. It's a complete revision and update of my first book, "Everybody Has A Tumor: Cures for the negative thoughts that are cancerous to our lives," which I published in 2000.

This revision became necessary when over the past four years my personal growth had refined my ideas so much that many of the principles in the original version no longer matched my way of thinking. Not to mention, I had generated so much new and powerful material that I simply had to get it out to the public.

My greatest innovation to date that is being released to the public for the first time in this book is the **Life Team Strategy**^{TM}. This strategy is one of the most profound, complete and yet simple methods for balancing your life. As the foundation of this book, the **Life Team Strategy**^{TM} will not only guide you through the book, but it will very likely begin to change the way you think before you've even reached the first chapter. Here's to you and the very best that life has to offer.

Introduction

An intricate web binds all of us together, each strand connecting one life to all others. This connection is best demonstrated in a concept referred to as the "butterfly effect." Simply put, since all of life is inextricably interconnected, if a butterfly in the central United States suddenly flaps its wings, you will see rain fall in New York where clear skies were previously predicted. I can't tell you how many times I've seen a meteorologist completely dumbfounded when some unforeseeable force comes out of nowhere and turns his or her beloved forecast on its head.

I don't mention the butterfly effect in order to offer a new method for weather prediction. I present it to you because it embodies a very important life principle: Even the slightest action—physical, verbal or even mere thought—can create profound change. It then stands to reason that when more action is taken, even greater change can take place.

History is filled with evidence of profound change that can come from a single action. Think of the change that came about with the uttering of such phrases as, "Let my people go," or "I have a dream." Think of how one man's single decision to become a doctor led to the cure for polio. Even more simple than that, how powerful the phrase "I love you" can be to someone whose day was changed for the better after hearing it.

Profound change often begins with single actions, which include decisions. In this book I will recommend many actions that can be taken to create profound change in your life immediately.

When each of us is being nourished by our mother's womb, we are like a chrysalis, undergoing profound transformation with growth as the only objective. Then during the miraculous process of birth, we break out of that world into a brand-new life, a new freedom with unlimited possibilities.

Most of us, however, slowly begin to wrap ourselves up in a new cocoon. As we are introduced to limiting people and limiting beliefs, we often choose to believe and accept the limitations we perceive—a straightjacket of our own creation. We end up going through life guided more by rules that hold us back than those that set us free. It is time to break out.

As with birth and the emerging of the monarch butterfly from its cocoon, there comes a point when we receive the signal to shed the straightjacket that is the only thing remaining between us and a new life. This signal, or inspiration for transformation, compels us to rediscover and recover the unlimited world we once knew.

As we begin our journey in this book, I will be discussing at great length my personal battle with a physical cancer. However, this book is not just about physical cancer; it is about the psychological and emotional cancers that are nurtured daily by our choices. We are often confronted by people, places and things as well as beliefs, attitudes and memories that compel us to limit our thinking, our options and eventually our movement through life.

Imagine you took a screwdriver and used it to twist a screw into a piece of wood so tightly that you couldn't get it back out again. That screw would be **Totally Screwed**. We often put ourselves in similar circumstances when our thinking is so limited that we render ourselves absolutely stuck. We limit our options and sabotage our ability to alter our own course. When we do this we are **Totally Screwed**. Keep in mind that being stuck so completely is just a perception—not reality. When you feel that you can't back yourself out of the hole you've screwed yourself into, then it's time to get rid of the screwdriver that got you there in the first place and use one or more different tools, different options, different choices. Options are precisely what this book will give. So welcome to Unscrew U!

I went from a life filled with self-imposed limitations to one that is limitless. The physical cancer was the major turning point in my life—my inspiration for transformation. The difficulty I had in dealing with the challenges that arose from having cancer compelled me to change the way I thought about and thus lived my life. It is these challenges that you need to focus on while reading my story. Concentrate on the transformation.

Those who've reached the point in their lives where a significant change is necessary are inspired to transform for many reasons: bankruptcy, divorce, death of a loved one or any other event that serves as an inspiration for transformation. If this is something you face, as you read my story, allow yourself to see what is inspiring your change. Once you identify it, you will be better able to embrace the techniques to help transform your life.

By practicing and implementing the techniques I have learned through my own experience in overcoming adversity, I discovered the cures for what ailed me. I was able to achieve a greater sense of mastery and balance in my everyday life. I believe they can have the same benefit for you. My cancer experience was the driving force that helped me become the person I am today. As I tell my story I use as much detail as possible to give you the feeling of being right along side me

Please Visit www.LifeTeamStrategy.com

as I endure the various struggles placed before me. My experiences were intense and overwhelming, and yet they were endurable, and life was even better when they were overcome. If I can survive struggles of this magnitude, I can survive anything, and so can you.

One final note before we begin. Many people who've taken the risk to dramatically change their lives have done so in response to a powerful inspiration for transformation; others responded to situations that were not so powerful. It is basically something that made change more desirable and more necessary than complacency. The better you understand your inspiration, the easier it will be to begin. The caterpillar is able to transform into a butterfly because it understands itself as a caterpillar. But keep in mind that you don't need to know absolutely everything about yourself at the outset. So be prepared to uncover things you didn't know were there. Even in a caterpillar's transformation there are things that take care of themselves by virtue of going through the process, but you will become aware that they are changing and you must commit to the process. Are you ready to become **Unscrewed**? Then it's time to begin.

Please Visit www.LifeTeamStrategy.com

Introducing, Your Life Team

Now that you understand what it means to be **Totally Screwed**, I want to introduce you to the simple concept I developed that is the key to helping you become **Unscrewed:** the **Life Team Strategy**™. The fact of the matter is that life occurs in a team environment and nobody makes it alone. I've always had an issue with concepts such as "The self-made man" or the notion of someone accomplishing something "all by themselves." These ideas are ludicrous for two reasons: First, they suggest that a person accomplishes his or her goals in a vacuum without any external influence, and second, they support the idea that it's important to succeed without anyone's help.

Anyone who's ever succeeded at anything has done so at least in part with the help of someone or something else. Although Thomas Edison conducted his experiments alone, he was not the inventor of the equipment he used to conduct those experiments. He needed the equipment and the people who made them as well as the people who made the material to make the equipment and so on. In addition to this tangible support, Edison also had help from an intangible source—his attitude. We'll talk more about this throughout the book, but I want you to start thinking about **attitude as a resource and as a teammate**.

As I said previously, "Life occurs in a team environment." We depend upon external as well as internal factors for our success. Our team is comprised of people, places and things on the exterior, and thoughts, beliefs, and attitudes on the interior. (*For the sake of brevity I'll refer to people and thoughts interchangeably with exterior and interior from now on*). Our exterior and interior depend on each other: When one is out of balance so is everything else. This book will teach you how to determine what's out of balance in your life and how to get it back in balance in the simplest of ways.

Our ability to grow and succeed depends entirely on the quality of our team of people and thoughts. Yes, thoughts are teammates just as much as people are, and just like people, we can pick and choose our thoughts. We choose our teammates based upon what they can do to contribute to the experiences we want to create in our lives. Before we can begin to choose the teammates we need, however, we need to understand the different attributes of the various types of teammates. Remember that exterior teammates are people, places and things that originate outside of us; interior teammates such as thoughts, perceptions and choices originate from within us.

Our **Life Team** is thus comprised of the following people and thoughts: **Starters**, **Sitters** and **Sneezers** on one side and **Shovers** and **Shouters** on the other side. I don't believe in types of people nor in labeling others, so these labels only refer to behaviors—not people. Let's take a look at the attributes of each team member.

Starters on the exterior are the first-string players on the team, the first ones in the game. They are the people that play at the same level you do or better. Starters are people you can count on to give you the resources you need to succeed in accomplishing your goals. They are often able to mentor you and help you become better. You want to make a major point in your life to surround yourself with these people as they are the key to helping you grow and succeed in life. A **Starter** on the interior is motivated and goal and action oriented. Remember this next point as you read the remainder of this book: The key attribute of a **Starter** is the unquenchable desire to accomplish a goal they've set their sights on. Without a desire this strong, you might as well stop now. Without this desire you will never rise above the level of a **Sitter**.

Sitters on the exterior are the second-string players who start the game on the bench—and for good reason. They are the people who are all pumped up to succeed and talk a good game, but when it comes time to deliver on the talk they fail to deliver. **Sitters** on the interior often lack adequate motivation or overestimate their true abilities.

Sneezers on the exterior are the cheerleaders on your team—those people who are always offering encouragement. They offer praise to your face or to other people. They are great for the pep talk, but they are not in a position to run out onto the field and give you a hand. On the interior, a **Sneezer** extends compliments to you and acknowledges your successes in a reasonable way. A Sneezer would say, "You're fantastic at such and such" or "Hey, that was a great job!"

Shovers on the exterior are the members of the opposing team and are either in competition with you or act in such a way to interfere with your best interests. Through specific action or inaction a **Shover** prevents you from acquiring the resources you need. At work a **Shover** could be a coworker who's competing for the same promotion. They might also be a supervisor who institutes unfair policy that makes your job more difficult. In a family, a **Shover** is most easily depicted by sibling rivalry. **Shovers** on the interior hold two contradictory beliefs simultaneously, such as the desire to achieve goals as well as the fear of failure.

Shouters on the exterior can be thought of as the fans of the opposing team and are the opposite of the **Sneezers**. A **Shouter** can be a person who simply does or says something intentionally or unintentionally with complete disregard for your feelings. **Shouters** either speak down to you from a sense of superiority or speak from a place of fear due to their own insecurity. **Shouters** differ from **Shovers** in that they can't directly interfere with your ability to achieve your goals, but they can mess with your head. Worst case scenario: A **Shouter** will do their damndest to convince you that you're not worthy of a goal. The worst of the **Shouters** want to encourage you to look at the negative side of things. It is in their best interest for you to give up. Unfortunately, **Shouters** are often the people who are closest to us.

A **Shouter** can often give you mixed messages of support and discouragement. For example, do you have people in your life who discourage you from thinking too big because they're afraid you'll be disappointed? Is there someone you know who worries and always looks at the dark side of things? They tell you they worry because they love you and smother you so that nothing bad happens to you. If these people and their thinking ever rub off on you, then they are contributing to your negative outcomes. **Shouters** on the interior criticize, doubt or place blame on themselves. These kinds of thoughts will interfere with an action-oriented mindset because they undermine your ability to achieve your goals.

The people in your life can play one, a few or all of these roles at varying times. For example, someone who's successful in business but lousy in love could be a great **Starter** in terms of business advice but could likely be a **Shouter** in terms of relationship advice. It's also important to understand that you can switch roles on yourself as well. You may believe wholeheartedly in yourself in one instance and doubt yourself in another—again going from **Starter** to **Shouter**.

Now that you're getting a sense of what each player contributes to your life, take some time to list the players you currently have on your Life Team. Make a list of those people that are **Starters, Sitters, Sneezers, Shovers** or **Shouters**. If you can, make sure you list an example of what they say or do that qualifies them in each role. Remember that each person can hold multiple positions. The power of doing this allows you to determine who you can count on for one thing and where you need to stay away from their input on another.

I had the client who inspired this model make the above list, and she determined that she was the only **Starter** on her team. The rest were either **Sneezers**

Please Visit www.LifeTeamStrategy.com

or **Shouters**. After realizing the serious imbalance in her support system, she also realized that she had been trying for years to convert the **Sneezers** and **Shouters** into **Starters**—and they were not looking to be converted! She wanted their support and assistance, but they only offered discouragement.

Once you realize what role a person is playing on your Life Team, don't waste your time and energy trying to change them into something they're not. If they want to move from **Sitter** to **Starter,** they'll do it in they're own time. If they're excellent **Sneezers,** be grateful for their Sneezing instead of exhausting and frustrating yourself by trying to get them to become **Starters** as well.

Once my client learned this lesson she realized she needed to look outside her immediate circle to recruit members for her team. What she quickly learned was that she was surrounded by people who were ready and willing to be her teammates, but because she was so busy trying to convert **Shouters** and waiting for the **Sneezers** to run onto the field, she ignored those who were ready to help her win.

Everyone in your life for the most part fits into one of these roles in terms of how they support your pursuit of personal growth and success. Once you understand where everybody fits, you understand exactly what you can expect from them and what you can't.

Understanding the Life Team Strategy^{TM} is essential if you're going to get anything out of the remainder of this book. A person becomes "Totally Screwed" when their Life Team is so out of whack that it doesn't support them adequately enough to grow as a human being. For example, when you have more **Shovers** and **Shouters** than you do **Starters**, you're life is out of balance. That goes for your thinking as well. When you spend more time **Shouting** at yourself than **Starting**, you are screwing yourself. The way to bring your life into balance is to tip the scale of your Life Team and make it heavy in terms of **Starters** and **Sneezers**.

The greater you can understand and apply the Life Team Strategy^{TM} to your thinking and your life, the more readily and quickly you'll be able to achieve the balance in life that you so richly deserve. Right now I have so many **Starters** on my team that the **Sitters** are permanently benched, the **Shovers** are battered and bruised and the **Shouters** have laryngitis. But it wasn't always that way.

The remainder of this book will take you to where it all started for me. I will tell you the story of how my Life Team was shattered, why it was shattered and how I put it back together again to create a balanced life for myself. I will tell you how I became Totally Screwed and then Unscrewed myself. In the end, you'll know how to do the same thing.

Please Visit www.LifeTeamStrategy.com

Keep in mind that there is no step-by-step method for restoring balance to your life through the Life Team Strategy^{TM} because everyone has constructed their life differently. What this book offers is observations and opportunities to look at your life through a unique lens that will hopefully provide more clarity in terms of the choices you've made and consequences you experience. I will also provide strategies throughout this book that you can apply to begin to see a major shift in how your life looks and feels. In order for any of the information in this book to be useful, however, you must make one decision and not waver from it: When it comes to your life, you must be prepared to lead and not follow. You are the greatest **Starter** you will ever have; you decide what you're going to do and when you're going to do it. You must be committed to doing right by yourself; otherwise, you will continue to screw yourself over and over again. But one thing is clear: If you weren't capable of being the **Starter** I know you can be, you never would have picked up this book. Now think of what an incredible **Starter** you'll be by the time you finish! Let's get started.

Please Visit www.LifeTeamStrategy.com

PART I
From Darkness to Light

"Doubt closes your eyes and darkens them to the possibilities. Hope opens them up again."

1

My Story of Adversity

I was 18 years old when I was thrust into a period of chaos that I never could have imagined. Over the course of that year my life nearly disintegrated as I found myself getting screwed tighter and tighter into a situation I thought I'd never get out of. That year ended up being the defining point in my life. During it I was forced to reexamine who I had been, who I had become and who I needed to be. This is my story of adversity and ultimately my story of triumph.

THE JOURNEY BEGINS

All of my life I never thought anything really bad would happen to me. As long as I prayed, confessed my sins and led a good life, I believed all the bad things would befall the next guy. I never would have guessed that I would become the next guy.

It all began in the middle of my 18th year. I was a senior in high school at the time. I was lying in bed one night, trying to fall asleep, when a sharp pain shot into my abdomen. It felt as if I had just been kicked in the groin. The pain was so excruciating that I doubled over and shouted a popular four-letter word that starts with an F and ends with a K and it wasn't "FORK!" The pain felt like it started in my right testicle. When I checked it I found that there was a very tender lump near the top of the testicle. I knew my body well enough to know that this was something new and didn't belong there. I felt I should have it looked at.

As Murphy's Law dictates, this problem dealt with a part of my anatomy that I wasn't comfortable discussing openly. However, urgent need for action superceded my fear of embarrassment, so I walked upstairs to my parents' bedroom. When given permission to enter, I spoke quickly to facilitate a fast exit. I told my mother I had a bump on my right testicle and it hurt very badly. I said I thought it would be a good idea to see a doctor. She looked at me, somewhat surprised, and simply said, "Okay." I suspect there isn't a passage in the parents handbook for how to respond to the statement I had just made. I closed their bedroom door and went back to my room. As I lay in bed I tried to relax and kept thinking to myself, "It's nothing, it's nothing." I was finally able to fall asleep.

Before I awoke the following morning, my mom had already made an appointment with our family physician, Dr. H. I didn't tell my siblings why I was going to the doctor because I felt a little strange and self-conscious about the nature of my problem. Once there I explained to the doctor what had happened the night before. She asked me a series of questions about the pain when it occurred to me that I had felt periods of discomfort a month prior. I experienced an achy feeling in my groin that would last a day or two, all the time varying in intensity. I didn't notice any lump when I examined myself then, and the pain eventually went away so I wrote it off as the typical growing pains of an 18-year-old. It wasn't until this lump suddenly showed up with this excruciating pain that I felt compelled to have it checked out.

The doctor examined the lump. It was round and about the size of a pea. "Ouch!" I shouted as she pressed on it, causing pain to again shoot into my abdomen. The pain throbbed for a few minutes, and I began feeling a little sick to my stomach. The doctor said it felt like it might be a cyst, but that a cyst would not typically be so painful. She said she didn't want to take any chances, so she went to the phone and called a colleague of hers named Dr. N. who was a pediatric urologist. She went into **Starter** mode and told him what she had found and said, "I don't care who you have to bump off your schedule. You have to see this kid tomorrow."

I went home and spent the rest of the day feeling anxious and impatient. I was aware of the pain more than ever, which only made it worse. As stressful as it was to have to wait until the next day for an answer to my problem, what choice did I have? First thing in the morning on the next day I was in Dr. N's office.

He examined me as the previous doctor had and arrived at the same conclusions, which brought about the same concerns. He wanted to have an ultrasound exam of my right testicle performed to determine whether the lump was a cyst or not. Unfortunately, the local hospital where he was on staff had no openings for two weeks. He could have been more of a **Starter** by pushing for an earlier appointment. Instead, I would have to wait. I quietly began to develop fears of what the lump might be. Every time I had heard the term lump used in relation to a body part, it was inevitably followed by the word "cancer." I kept telling myself that if cancer was a possibility then the doctors wouldn't wait; they'd be concerned and want to act sooner. I continually went through the rationalizing song and dance of it couldn't happen to me anyway because these things only happen to other people. With this I did my best to quiet my fears because I didn't

Please Visit www.LifeTeamStrategy.com

want to worry until there was something to worry about. So I kept my fingers crossed, rooted for a cyst and tended to my schoolwork and other life matters—all the while trying not to think about it. Easier said than done, especially because the lump was still pretty painful.

Occasionally the lump would begin to throb again, which made me inclined to check it each time (in private of course). As the days passed the lump felt like it was getting bigger. It gradually lost its smooth surface and assumed a bumpier more irregular one. As it got more uncomfortable and I got more anxious, I kept telling myself, "It's nothing, it's nothing."

Nothing was the only thing I could handle it being. When the day of the ultrasound finally arrived, I asked my mother to go with me for support. If it turned out to be something, I didn't want to be alone when I found out. Fortunately, my mother had already decided that nothing would keep her from being there with me.

Once at the hospital, I was taken to the examining room, and Dr. N., the urologist, appeared. I had had a lot of tests in the past for various reasons, and this was the first time any doctor of mine had shown up for it. I didn't know if this was a good sign or a bad one; in either case, it was a very **Starter** thing for him to do. He asked me how I was doing, and I told him that I felt the lump was getting bigger.

He proceeded to examine my testicle again and observed that the lump seemed to have doubled in size since he had seen me two weeks earlier. The expression on his face didn't change, which to me meant he wasn't feeling any overwhelming concern at this development (either that or he had a stellar poker face). I thought for an instant that maybe I was overreacting and this is just what cysts do. But then he turned to the technologist who was to perform the test and asked if she wouldn't mind if he had another doctor do the exam. He briefly left the room and returned with Dr. B., the head of the radiology department. He performed the exam as he and my doctor viewed the images on a small video monitor. They maintained convincing poker faces as they pointed at the screen and made little comments about what they were seeing. Their demeanor led me to believe that nothing in what they were seeing was of any real concern.

After the two doctors completed the exam, Dr. N. asked me to sit in the waiting room where he would come talk to my mother and me in a few minutes. I remember telling my mom that it was probably nothing. Not much later Dr. N. came out and spoke to us. He told us he had reviewed the films with the other doctor and they had concluded that the lump in my testicle didn't appear to be a fluid filled cyst after all but, in fact, appeared to have a solid mass to it. Considering the fact that it was growing, it needed to be surgically removed as soon as possible. I felt my heart start racing as my thoughts of "It's nothing" quickly changed to "What is it?"

Again the word "cancer" started running through my head, but I didn't say anything. I really didn't know what to say. My mom asked if it could wait a few weeks because I would be graduating high school soon. Dr. N. said absolutely not, that it was imperative to get this taken care of immediately. We agreed, and he arranged for surgery to take place in two days.

During those couple of days I became very task oriented. I would be having surgery on a Wednesday and would have to remain in the hospital until Friday. I concerned myself with school and getting the assignments I would miss so I could work on them in the hospital. I studied whether I felt I needed to or not just to keep my mind occupied. I slept surprisingly well the night before the operation.

After I checked in with the receptionist at the hospital, she took me to a dressing room. It would have been more appropriate to call it an undressing room because I had to remove all of my clothes and put a gown on that was open in back such that all of my secrets could be revealed to the world. I hardly felt dressed at all. I might as well have been at a nudist colony initiation.

When I was comfortably "dressed" in my oversized designer tissue, the receptionist sat me down with a lengthy release form to fill out before surgery. It asked for my permission for any of a list of things to take place during surgery. I became very nervous because I thought all of things would take place if I signed it. Just then Dr. N. showed up. He would be performing the surgery and wanted to know if I had any questions. I told him I was concerned about the things I had just read. He told me that the items listed were only possibilities, not routine occurrences. The first thing I asked was if it was okay for me to cross out items that I was uncomfortable with, especially the part about the possibility that video cameras might be present in the operating room to film the procedure for educational purposes. The last thing I wanted was my crotch on PBS; although, I'm sure the program would have won awards, especially for me as Best Actor in an Unconscious Role. He said it was perfectly all right to cross that out. He then sat down beside me, and we went through the form together.

He asked if I had any other questions, and there was only one on my mind: "Are you going to have to take my testicle out?" He said he wouldn't know for sure until he saw what we were dealing with, but probably. I asked him to do his best to leave it intact. I had had it since birth after all and had become rather attached to it and it to me. He then said he'd see me in a little while and left to

Please Visit www.LifeTeamStrategy.com

prepare for surgery. I was then asked to lie down on a cart and was wheeled into a holding area where I was left to wait for a minute or two.

A young man walked in wearing a surgical cap and scrubs. He had a small bowl filled with soapy water in one hand and a small razor in the other. I could tell he sensed the awkwardness of the moment as he told me that it was his job to shave me before surgery—and he wasn't referring to my face. He proceeded to lift the front of my scanty gown and went to work. We made very little eye contact as we engaged in light chitchat to get through the few minutes that it took, after which he covered me back up, wished me luck and left.

I was moved once again and briefly parked outside the door of the operating room where my surgery was to take place. A nurse came out with a syringe and said she had to give me a shot of a substance to make my mouth dry so I wouldn't be inclined to swallow and possibly vomit during surgery. That seemed very reasonable to me. Then the anesthesiologist came out and told me he was going to start an IV in my arm so he could administer the anesthesia. I turned my head away and could have sworn I heard a pop as I felt the sharp pain of the needle sliding into my arm. He told me when he was beginning to run the anesthesia, and no sooner had he said that that I felt the lights go out.

Then next thing I remember was hearing a lady's voice calling my name as I fought to open my eyes. I finally managed to pry them open, and as they slowly came into focus, the first thing I saw was Dr. N's comforting face looking down into my eyes. What a **Starter**. I later thanked him for that because there's nothing like coming out of a frightening experience and seeing a familiar face. I was still half sedated but was able to muster the strength to ask him in a groggy voice, "Is it gone?" With a consoling look he nodded his head. "Oh no" I said while shaking my head. He patted me on the knee and said he would come up to my hospital room in about an hour to see me. He had made a good-sized incision in my abdomen to remove the testicle and wanted me to stay a few days to make sure it was healing well before releasing me.

THE DIAGNOSIS

Dr. N. came to my room a while later where my mother and I were waiting. He asked how I was feeling, and I was feeling quite well, all things considered. Actually I was indulging in some hefty denial. I wasn't prepared to deal with the loss of my testicle. I viewed it as an assault upon my masculinity. As I gripped my mother's hand he told us he had been to the lab where my testicle had been sent

Please Visit www.LifeTeamStrategy.com

for testing. Before he could say anything else my mother asked if it was cancer. He nodded and said, "Yes." I remember my stomach dropping and my mind going blank. "I'm dead," I thought to myself.

He went on to explain that it appeared the tumor had been growing for some time inside the testicle, which was why I had felt some discomfort over the past month. It wasn't until it got so large that it ran out of room and began to push against the wall of the testicle that it created a lump, which could be noticed. The reason it had hurt so much was that it was growing by the major blood supply to that testicle and was drawing so much blood that it began to hemorrhage. If it hadn't done that I may not have discovered the lump until it was too late. Talk about luck. He reassured us that he believed he had removed all of the cancerous cells but wanted me to come back in a month for a post-surgical blood test to confirm it.

Just like that my worst fear had been confirmed and relieved in almost an instant. Even though he had said he'd gotten it all, I had a hard time letting go of the news I'd just received. I had cancer. Even if it was gone, the fact that it had been there at all was terrifying. I still felt that I was diseased somehow and was afraid to feel relieved only to be hit with the news again. I wasn't sure what to do with myself. I didn't know whether to relax or panic. Either way I had a lot I would have to adjust to, and my life was obviously going to be quite different from this point forward.

It wasn't until later that night after my mom had left that I checked myself for the first time. It was a strange feeling to know that some part of my body had just been removed. But why did it have to be this part? I was an 18-year-old male and insecure enough about my manhood as it was. I was afraid to touch my scrotum because I didn't know if it would hurt or not. I gently touched it, and it actually felt normal—normal but partially empty. It seemed so weird feeling only one testicle where there had previously been two. I really couldn't tell it was gone until I checked it. I thought it would be as noticeable as if I had lost a limb or something. Physically I couldn't sense that anything had changed. Mentally was another story.

I had been raised in a social environment that was overflowing with a river of immature male testosterone. Unfortunately, in my world, the male mentality was based on the superiority of their own equipment and making others feel insecure about theirs. However irrational this preoccupation might have been, it was my only point of reference for forming my self-image. For this reason I began to feel inadequate—like part of my manhood had been taken away. Even worse was the embarrassment I felt every time a nurse would come into my room to check my incision. I knew how I'd learned to judge the measure of a man and was afraid these nurses judged according to the same standard. I stopped counting the number of times I felt myself turning red.

I did my best not to deal with the loss at that time. Instead I tried to keep my mind focused on school by attempting to complete the work I'd brought with me. With all the pain medication I was being given, geometry wasn't the easiest thing to do. Needless to say, I didn't get very much done. My mother came and stayed with me everyday. So when I wasn't struggling with my studies, her company provided more than a sufficient alternative to dealing with my insecurities. After three days I was allowed to go home. I was able to rest through the weekend before going back to school. I soon found out that I would not be returning to life as I knew it.

MY FRIENDS RECEIVE THE NEWS

When I arrived at school the news of my diagnosis was already well circulated. My younger sister, who was also in high school at the time, and my girlfriend were openly voicing their concerns about my health to others. I was so self-conscious about my missing testicle that it was all I could think about. It was now common knowledge where my cancer had been found and that I had been physically compromised. I subconsciously feared how others might judge me, and I consciously feared people lining up to stare at my crotch like I was wearing a shirt that read "Take a Number."

Not knowing how to deal with the immense insecurity I was feeling, I decided I would just try and put it all behind me and attempt to get back to normal. It quickly became apparent that normal wasn't looking to get back to me. I began noticing a change in how my peers related to me. Except for a slight limp from the pain of my incision, outwardly I appeared unchanged. I had lost a testicle, which I would have to learn to deal with. Beyond that I didn't feel any different. I kept telling myself that as far as I was concerned, the cancer was gone and I had nothing to worry about, so I was going to continue as I had before.

My closest friends didn't treat me differently at first because they knew I was okay with everything. But others looked at me like they where surprised I was still breathing. I kept getting questions like "Are you okay?" or "Are you going to die?" I was so shocked by the boldness of the question that I was tempted to say, "I could go at any second, so you'd better back up so I don't land on you." Instead I replied, "I'm fine. The doctor thinks he got it all." "Good, good" they would say and then walk away. They tried to be **Starters,** but some ended up being **Shouters**. Under the circumstances I'm not sure what I would have said if I were in their shoes.

At the time I thought to myself, what's wrong with these people? The most shocking of all was how some of my "friends" stopped talking to me altogether. They seemed to go from **Starter** to **Sitter,** and I couldn't understand why they had this reaction. I told them that I had had cancer, and upon hearing this, some of them just gave me a blank stare and walked away. What was up with that? What was the problem? I'm fine now. I decided I just needed to blow them off because I had final exams and graduation to worry about. I would have to talk to them at another time.

The remaining few weeks of school were very difficult. I hadn't been able to study in the hospital because the morphine I was getting for pain made it difficult to concentrate. The painkillers I was given to take at home made me drowsy, and my final exam grades reflected that. I had gotten A's and B's until that point, so I wasn't hurt that bad academically. I still wish I could have done better.

ONE LAST HURRAH

Well, graduation came and went, and I was free to pursue my life. I began thinking once again as any 18 year old would. I was planning on a long, fun-filled summer, after which I would enroll in my local community college to begin studies in psychology. But before I could dive into the rest of my life, I had one last piece of high school business to take care of. I had been involved in my school's anti-drug and alcohol clown troupe. We would put on makeup and funny clothes and travel to area grade schools to perform original skits about the dangers of drug and alcohol use.

I was celebrating my last hurrah with the troupe in the Fourth of July parade for one of the surrounding communities. I remarked to one of my teammates, "I'd better enjoy this because this is probably going to be the last time I put on makeup." It turns out that my statement couldn't have been further from the truth.

During October of the previous year, I had auditioned for a school that I felt I had no hope of getting into, but I tried out anyway in response to peer and family encouragement. The audition was for acceptance into Ringling Brothers and Barnum and Bailey Circus Clown College, which at the time was located in Venice,

Please Visit www.LifeTeamStrategy.com

Florida. On the morning after the parade, my dad woke me up and said that Clown College was on the phone.

I jumped out of bed and quickly made my way to the kitchen. I picked up the phone and on the other end was Steve Smith, the Dean of Clown College at the time. He said the reason he was calling was not only to inform me that I was accepted and to invite me to attend, but also to tell me that I had been accepted unanimously by the board of directors, which almost never happens. He asked if I would have any problems attending. "Of course not!" I told him and thanked him profusely.

A chance to try out for "The Greatest Show on Earth." A chance to travel all over the country as a clown in a big top circus. I could barely contain myself. For the past few weeks since graduation, I had been having problems with my wisdom teeth. I didn't want to have problems with them while I was away, so I had all four of them removed. They were all impacted so the doctor had to saw into my jaw to get them out. As a result, my mouth swelled shut and my face looked like a squirrel with a mouth full of nuts. I had two weeks to go before my flight, and it was now time for the follow-up blood test to my surgery. It was a simple procedure. I went to the hospital to have my blood drawn and went on my way.

NOT SO FAST

A few days later Dr. N. called and spoke to my mother. He said he wanted me to have another blood test because he thought the lab might have made a mistake. When my mom asked why, he said the numbers in the resulting measurements seemed too high, and he wanted another test to make sure. When she told me, I thought nothing of it. So they made a mistake—it happens. I had more blood drawn and went about my business. Another few days passed, and Dr. N. called back. I was out with my friends when my mother received the call.

He explained to her that before my surgery, blood was drawn to determine the levels of a certain protein in my blood, which is used to determine the presence of my type of cancer. Fortunately, the levels were only slightly elevated at 9 from a normal range of 4 to 8. Immediately after surgery, more blood was taken that revealed the level of that protein was normal and that cancer was no longer present. He was concerned when he received the results of the recent follow-up test because the number was now 15—which was why he suspected an error had been made. But he had just received my most recent test results, which were taken only a few days after the first test, and now the number was 35. He said there was no mistake—my cancer was back and growing quickly.

Dr. N informed my mother that before he had called her, he had called several cancer centers all over the country to find out the best place to send me. The responses he got were unanimous, so I would be venturing to a hospital in Indiana. A doctor there was testing an experimental protocol on testicular cancer and was having great success with it. Dr. N. had just exemplified the **Starter** position when it came to my well-being. My mother then phoned the hospital in Indiana and was told to have me there in 24 hours to begin chemotherapy.

I got home late that night, and my father asked my mother to let me get a good night's sleep before breaking the news. Nothing was going to happen right then anyway. I later asked my mother how she and Dad slept that night, and she blurted out, "Like shit." They spent most of the time talking about how to keep everything together for the next week while she was with me in Indiana. The next morning they entered my room together. I was still half asleep when they dropped the bomb. After taking a few seconds to comprehend what they'd said, I jumped out of bed and said, "Okay let's go get this over with."

My parents broke the news to my siblings shortly after they told me. When my 15-year-old sister Melissa heard the news she burst into tears and threw her arms around me saying, "I don't want you to die." All I could do in return was to reassure her that everything would be all right. I was touched by her reaction since she'd spent most of her life wishing I'd never been born. My brother Chris was doubly screwed that day because in addition to the news that my cancer had returned it was also his 20th birthday.

I walked around in shock at first, but the problem had been remedied with such relative ease before that I thought it would only take a few days again. All I knew was I was leaving for Clown College in a week and had to get this out of the way. How naïve I was. Mom said I was going to receive chemotherapy treatments. I had no idea what was in store for me. My mother was going to drive me to Indiana, so we spent the better part of the day packing for our trip. My father would have to stay behind to run the family business.

It took four hours to get there from our home in a Chicago suburb. I spent the trip looking at the scenery and spotting out-of-state license plates. Anything I could do to keep my mind off where we were going and what we were going for. I just wanted it over with already. We were fortunate enough to reserve a room in a hotel across the street from the hospital. I was tired from the trip, so I was able to sleep relatively well that night. The next morning we had an early breakfast so I could be at the hospital by 7 a.m. as they had requested. When it was about ten minutes until seven, we paid the waitress and walked across the street. I still really hadn't taken any of this seriously. I thought I'd get some medicine and go home.

ROUND ONE

We walked to the information desk, and my mother barely uttered my name to the woman sitting there before she quickly jumped from her seat. With a look of urgency she said, "Oh yes we heard you were coming."

She called someone on the phone, and not a minute later a man flew around the corner with a wheelchair and whisked me away with my mother in tow. I was taken into a back room and asked to sit in a chair with an armrest that looked like one you'd find in a classroom. Two nurses were in there bouncing around the room, frantically getting supplies. At the time I thought they were in a hurry because they had other things to do. Then one of them came over and started an IV in my arm. I asked her what she was giving me. I was surprised when she told me it was the chemotherapy.

I didn't know what chemotherapy was. I didn't know it came in a plastic bag. Just as she was finishing, the door to the room opened and a small, thin gentleman wearing slacks and a dress shirt entered the room. There was a large entourage behind him. He introduced himself as Dr. E. and explained that he would be overseeing my treatment. Dr. E. was the primary **Starter** on my medical team who had devised the treatment I'd be receiving. He said the hospital had had a lot of success with my type of cancer, and he was confident they could get rid of it for me. He then left, and two younger doctors from his group remained and began writing prescriptions for drugs to relieve various side effects of the chemotherapy.

With the chemo well underway, I was taken for a CAT scan, where I was made to drink two large cups of an iodine-based liquid dye mixed with fruit flavoring that might as well have been battery acid. The gag reflex it brought about in my throat was unrivaled in the history of modern nausea. I drank as much as I could and was then escorted into the exam room where I lied on the moveable table of the CAT scan machine. It was there that they injected a second dye into my arm to top off what I had drunk. The subsequent exam revealed that my cancer had indeed spread and had formed a large tumor in one of my abdominal lymph nodes.

The roller coaster ride had begun with no sign of stopping anytime soon. After several other tests, which lasted almost all day, I was finally taken up to my room.

Please Visit www.LifeTeamStrategy.com

It wasn't until now that I was given the antinausea sedatives that were prescribed for me. They were powerful and hit me hard and fast. I became so loopy, for lack of a better word, that I started to forget where I was. I was attempting to relax after a horrible day when I quickly discovered what it meant to be a patient in a teaching hospital.

A medical student entered my room, whose infinite wisdom told him that my day just wouldn't be complete without a rectal exam—compliments of his index finger. This guy was a real **Shover,** and after the day I'd had this was the straw that broke the camel's back. Through heavy sedation and a mouth still swollen shut from my dental surgery, it was difficult to express the humiliation this complete stranger was putting me through. This act of inconsideration made my stomach turn. My mother was watching me, and her instincts made her painfully aware of what was coming next. A nurse entered the room, saw the student in action and quickly kicked him out, saying it was a bad time. As he left the room, my mother rushed to my bedside with a washing basin as I proceeded to vomit everything I'd eaten since I was five years old. With a mouth that's swollen shut this was not an easy task. It was similar to what would happen if you placed your thumb partially over the end of a hose while water was coming out. Although I remember this event quite vividly, I believe it would have been much worse had I not been so medicated. After that I fell asleep from exhaustion.

The next day went a little better. I was still pretty out of it from the medication, so my mom took to answering all of the staff's questions on my behalf. I couldn't remember basic things, like my age or the day of the week. I mostly slept. I had my mom call my girlfriend so she could be brought up to date. She had no idea of the magnitude of the situation, as she seemed unconcerned as I described to her what was happening.

That night I started feeling pretty lousy. The medication finally had my nausea under control, but I started feeling a strong pressure in my chest. My heart started beating really fast and really hard. It beat so hard I could feel it pounding against the inside of my chest, and each beat was more painful than the last. It was also getting harder and harder to breathe. When my mom came back from getting something to eat, I told her how I was feeling. She asked the nurse to check me, and then I remember being moved to another room so I could be given oxygen. Either that night or early the next morning I was taken to have an echocardiogram, an ultrasound exam of the heart. It turned out that my heart was fine. The doctors believed I was just having palpitations as an adverse reaction to the chemotherapy drugs. Whatever the reason, that feeling was nasty—and frightening. If having the feeling that your heart was going to explode is typical of this treatment, I was terrified of what other pleasantries were on the horizon. By the middle of the next day, the symptoms had eventually subsided but left me even more exhausted.

The following morning my mother woke me and said she was going to the airport to pick up my father. Apparently she had spoken to him the night before, and he told her that he couldn't bear not being there with us. He would be leaving my older brother, Chris, in charge of the family business for the next couple of days. My 15-year-old sister, Melissa, would have to miss at least a week of her summer vacation, as she was put in charge of sitting at the desk and fielding phone calls.

Not long after my mother left, I was able to fall back to sleep. A while later I heard a voice asking me to wake up. My eyes sprung open to see a room full of people in white lab coats, with Dr. E. standing in the middle. What a rude awakening! This is Mr. King, Dr. E. told the group, of whom I assumed were medical students. He briefly described the facts of my case to them, and they all turned and left the room without so much as a word to me. He'd spoken to them as though I were being presented as a diseased specimen and not a person. Dr. E. acted like a real **Shouter** right then. See how easily even the most important person can switch roles on you?

I was very insulted by this intrusion. I wondered why he couldn't just let them peak in the room without waking me and then discuss me later. It really left me with the perception that they weren't interested in me as a person. Beyond meeting him my first day, this brief visit was the only time I saw him the entire week I was there. He was overseeing my treatment but knew nothing about me personally, unlike Dr. N who was one of the most hands-on doctors I've ever known. I got the feeling that I was only a chart filled with symptoms and numbers to Dr. E. I was treated like a disease wrapped in a person, when what I really needed was to be treated like a person who happened to have a disease.

I learned that sleep for a patient in a hospital is a scarce commodity, because every time I started to get some, it was interrupted. Why does the staff insist on disturbing the few minutes of rest a patient is able to get? Sure, they had various tasks to accomplish, but it must have occurred to them at some point that lack of sleep might just be detrimental to the healing process. Alas, it didn't seem to matter to them. In this instance the hospital, which was overall a great **Starter,** had many policies that were **Shovers.** It might have helped if the doctor would have seen me and not just my chart. Maybe I could have asked him to allow me a little rest. In retrospect, though, I am able to put the feeling that I was disrespected

Please Visit www.LifeTeamStrategy.com

aside. Dr. E. did develop the treatment I received, so in light of this, any shortcomings I may have perceived in his care were miniscule.

One of the best memories I had of my stay there were the many visits I received from a nursing student named Honey F. Yes, that was her real name. She would tell jokes and do whatever it took to keep my spirits up. In spite of my condition she wouldn't tolerate my crabbiness. When Honey needed to be a **Starter** she really stepped up. She would inflate latex gloves, draw smiley faces on them and hang them from my IV pole. I'll admit it was very difficult to be a grump with her around.

Another time during that week my uncle Lou and his wife, Kathy, drove down to the hospital from their home in Central Illinois to offer their support. I remember when they came into my room. Lou went to my father and shook his hand, while Kathy gave my mother a big hug. Kathy then walked over to my bed and touched my hand as she asked how I was doing. I was so sedated I don't even remember giving her an answer. I have always been grateful for their gracious gesture, and I thank them both every time I get a chance. They were real **Starters** for my family that day.

The hardest day of the week was Sunday. This was the day I was supposed to be boarding a plane for Clown College. Instead I was lying in a hospital bed hundreds of miles from home. While other kids my age were enjoying their summers and preparing for their futures, I was here fighting for my life, wondering if I would even have a future.

The next day I received the last of the chemotherapy for that week and began preparing to go home. One of my nurses briefed my mother and me on the course of my treatment from this point on. She told me I would need a few more rounds of chemotherapy, but the doctor was going to arrange for another doctor at my local hospital to oversee my care. This meant I could finish my chemo near home. The nurse gave my mom information on my treatment and directions on taking care of me. She also gave my mom the name of the doctor who would be overseeing my treatment back home. I began feeling like I was being punished somehow. I felt cheated for not being able to go to Clown College and being forced to miss this tremendous opportunity, but I knew I clearly had bigger fish to fry.

I slowly staggered out of the hospital. My parents offered their help, but I wanted to walk by myself. I had been poked and prodded all week long. I wanted at least a few minutes of independence. Between the antinausea drugs and chemotherapy, I felt like I had gotten drunk and then had the crap kicked out of me by ten people. Needless to say the ride home was rough. Too weak to sit up, I laid in the back seat of the car. The antinausea drugs had begun to wear off, and it was impossible to keep my head from swimming and my stomach from turning during the four-hour drive home. I'm sure the drive was more like five or six hours because I kept asking my dad to pull over so I could regain my bearings to prevent myself from throwing up. When we finally got home the only thing I wanted to do was go to sleep in my own bed. With all the aches and pains I felt like I had the worst case of the flu in the world. Trying to get comfortable enough to get some sleep was difficult.

Hair Today, Gone Tomorrow

A few days later I went to the office of Dr. G. who would be overseeing the rest of my treatment. The thing I remember most about our meeting is when I asked him what the chances were that my hair would fall out—a side effect I heard was common with chemotherapy. He said about 90%. The loss of my hair would be a dramatic change in any case, but my hair was short on top like a flat top and reached the middle of my shoulder blades in back. Baldness would obviously be the polar opposite of that.

When we got back from the doctor. I said, "Mom I've got an idea. Before my hair falls out I want to go to a T-shirt shop and get a hat and shirt made that says, "CHEMO SUCKS!" My brother, Chris, chuckled at this notion, and my mom thought it was a neat idea, so off we went. I explained to the gentleman who was helping us why I wanted this, and he was more than happy to assist us. I got a matching shirt and baseball cap both dark blue in color with bold white letters ironed on them. I told my mom I would wear them like badges of honor.

That night my siblings went out with their friends, and my parents wanted to go out to dinner. But I wasn't up to it. My mom was reluctant to go because she wasn't comfortable leaving me alone. I assured her I would be fine. She gave me the name of the restaurant where they would be and gave me a hug and kiss, telling me they wouldn't be gone long.

I was sitting there watching television and remembered what the doctor had said about the probability of my hair falling out. Out of curiosity I ran my hand down the back of my head and grabbed a handful of the longest portion of my hair. I gently pulled but didn't feel any pulling on my scalp so I thought my hand was just running down the length of my hair. When I looked at my hand, my eyes sprung open. "Oh my God!" I said in shock.

Please Visit www.LifeTeamStrategy.com

I had a handful of hair that looked like I'd just cut a horse's tail off. I quickly walked to the bathroom and threw that handful in the garbage. I then sat on the edge of the toilet and kept pulling. I couldn't believe how easily it was all coming out. It was like it was all just sitting on my head completely unattached from my scalp. It was so loose that I didn't know how much had come out until I looked in my hand. This is outrageous, I kept thinking to myself. I kept pulling for the next hour or so until no more would come out. By the time I had finished, all that was left was two or three very thin tufts of hair on the front and back of my head. I was at least 95% bald. I hadn't looked in the mirror yet, but I could tell just by feeling my head how much was gone.

I was about to look when I heard my parents come through the front door. My mom called out and asked where I was. I heard her walking down the hall towards the bathroom. "Stop right there," I shouted before she could reach the door. "I want you to prepare yourself." "Are you bald?" she asked. She's always had tremendous instincts. "Yes, very," I replied. She slowly peaked around the corner and said, "Oh, that's not too bad." I stood up and looked in the mirror. "Oh my God!" I said again as my eyes sprung open with surprise. I looked like Charlie Brown. I was so amazed at how in just one hour it had all fallen out. No one had prepared me for that. I thought it was going to take weeks.

It was pretty late by then, and I'd had quite enough for one day, so I went to bed. My mom decided to check on me before she turned in for the night. She poked her head around the door and asked if I was okay. I told her I was fine.

It was hard to fall asleep at first because my head didn't feel quite right. The pillowcase was cold against my bare head. It wasn't until I had the idea of lying a towel over my pillow that I was finally able to fall asleep.

The next morning I woke up around nine o'clock and called my girlfriend "J." I told her about my dramatic change in appearance, to which she asked, "It'll grow back, right?" "Of course," I replied. She didn't seem too concerned after that.

I asked her if she wanted to go out and do something together. We decided to see a movie, and we invited my mother to come with us. My mom graciously agreed to serve as chauffer and ATM for that afternoon. The movie wasn't until later that day, but I went to pick up "J" early so we could spend some time together beforehand. When I arrived, her mother greeted me at the door and asked me how I was doing. "Fine," I said. "Nice hat," she remarked with a smirk on her face.

I went inside for a few minutes while "J" finished getting ready. While her mother and I sat on the couch talking, her six-year-old sister walked into the

Please Visit www.LifeTeamStrategy.com

room and sat down next to me. She looked at my head curiously and started reaching for my hat. I gently took her hand before she could take it off. As I did that she quietly asked, "Is your hair gone?" "Yes it is," I said. She asked where it had gone because she had seen me a week earlier with a full head of long hair.

I didn't know how to explain cancer and chemotherapy to her, so I searched my imagination quickly for an answer I thought she would understand. I asked her if she had squirrels in her yard. She replied that she did. I went on to explain that behind my house there is a big field with a lot of squirrels in it. Many of the squirrels used up all the grass and sticks to make their nests in the trees and left two of the squirrels without anything to make their nests with. So I went to them and told them they could use my hair because I had a lot of it, and it would grow back. "Really?" she asked with interest and a little bit of doubt. I think she half believed me. At that same time, my sweetheart had finished getting ready, so we left and headed back to my house to hang out until it was time to leave for the movie.

When we arrived, my mom greeted us and called to my sister, Melissa, who was still in her room. My mom told her to come see my new look. Melissa hadn't seen me since the day before when I still had hair, as I had gone to bed before she got home. When she came out, I was sitting on the couch next to "J" with my bald head covered by my CHEMO SUCKS! hat. All I said was, "Hi, sis." She took one look at me then covered her mouth with her hands as she said, "Oh my God." She burst into tears and ran back to her room. My mother and I looked at each other with surprise. "What happened?" I asked in shock. My mom went to Melissa's room to see if she was all right. I was startled by her reaction and even felt a little guilty for upsetting her. About a half-hour later Melissa came out of her room and gave me a hug. She said, "I'm not upset. I was shocked. I didn't expect to see that."

I told her I understood. A few hours later we left for the movies. Things went okay for the next couple of weeks. I spent most of my time at home and with my girlfriend. The people around me, my family mostly, seemed to be adjusting pretty well to the changes that were taking place. I hadn't spoken to anyone else yet about the fact that my cancer had returned because everything had happened too fast and I was more interested in staying close to home where I felt the most safe. It was now time to go to our local hospital to begin my next round of chemotherapy. During this next week is when my life began a rapid decline.

Round Two

The first round of chemotherapy had claimed the hair on my head, and I was also experiencing a progressive decline in my strength. Over the two weeks since I had left Indiana, I'd been able to regain a good amount of stability in my life again. As my mother drove me to the hospital, the memories of my previous hospital stay came flooding back, and I became very anxious. I was frightened of being violated again and quickly began to develop an attitude of defiance.

After arriving at the hospital and being admitted for treatment, my mom and I were directed to the room where I'd be staying. Ironically, as the elevator doors opened onto the floor I was to exit, there was Dr. G. waiting to get on. He paused and took one look at my CHEMO SUCKS! hat and shirt and busted out laughing. He then looked at my face and realized who I was. I did look considerably different from when he last saw me. He grabbed a fellow physician, who was standing nearby, and said, "You gotta see this kid."

They both had a good chuckle from the manner in which I chose to express my feelings. They both commended me for how well I hit the nail on the head. My doctor asked if he could borrow my hat for a few minutes to go show it to some other doctors. I didn't mind showing it off, so I let him take it. My mother retrieved it a little while later.

As I was getting comfortable (as much as possible) in my hospital bed, an attractive young lady walked in and introduced herself as Laura. She said she would be my nurse during the day for that week. I was a little testy that day, so when she asked if she could do anything for me, my response was, "You can undo your shirt one more button." My mom laughed, as she understood I was joking, but Laura's jaw dropped and her face turned beet red. I told her I was just joking, and my mother spoke to her later so she would take no offense. It turns out that no offense was taken. It was the bluntness of the remark that caught her off guard. I'm ashamed of what I said to her that day. It wasn't the best way to start things off with her. She was trying to be a **Starter**, and I acted like a **Shouter**. I guess this was just a juvenile attempt on my part to take charge of the situation. When she walked into the room I remembered how I felt the first time I was there after my testicle was removed and how insecure and embarrassed I felt every time a nurse entered the room. I suppose I got a little defensive. I quickly realized how much I would have to depend on her and changed my tune after that.

I tried to stay positive, but this was the week reality really began to hit me—and it really hit me hard. I was being given chemotherapy daily, and with each passing hour, I began to feel worse. Again, the antinausea drugs put me in a stupor that left me unable to comprehend much of what was going on around me. I would wake up each morning (if I'd slept) and find my sheets covered with hair. I was beginning to lose all of my body hair—and I do mean all. My eyebrows and eyelashes thinned, and whenever I blew my nose the hairs blew out as well. My sheets had to be changed a few times a day because I was shedding worse than a cat. I wasn't prepared for all of this, and I was quickly becoming extremely self-conscious, more ashamed, embarrassed and very angry. Everything was changing faster than I knew how to deal with.

It was impossible to sleep because my room was only a door down from the nurse's station, which was never quiet. Every hour or so someone would come in to check my IV and always moved my arm to do it. Then at five in the morning, every morning, someone came in and abruptly turned on the light to take my blood. Those damn **Shover** hospital policies again. This barrage of institutional inconsideration dealt by the hospital was wearing down my resolve. Between lack of sleep, the head-to-toe nausea and the constant poking and prodding, I began to feel like this whole process was against me.

I had been put into a hospital that was supposed to help me get better. Instead I was dressed in a gown that barely covered me and was embarrassing to wear, as I was forced to moon the world with every turn. I was denied sleep and all privacy. Nearly everyone who came through my door was a stranger who was there to administer pain or probe my body in a humiliating way. I felt like I had no say in my life anymore as I was repeatedly told by my nurses and doctors that I had to endure this treatment to get better.

The icing on the cake occurred during my fourth day there. I discovered that my regular nurse Laura was off when a nurse I didn't recognize came into my room and hung the bags of chemotherapy along with a few other medications on my IV pole. A few minutes later I began shaking uncontrollably and felt like I was freezing. I felt like the inside of my body was slowly turning to ice. I could literally feel cold flowing through my heart as I curled into a ball to try and stay warm. I began shaking so hard that I pulled several muscles in my legs and back. The pain from this only got worse because I couldn't stop shaking.

My mother walked in and saw what was happening. "What's wrong?" she asked in a worried voice. "I'm ffffffreezing," I told her. She brought the nurse in, and they began piling blankets on top of me, which did nothing to stop the freezing or the shaking. Noticing that I was currently receiving intravenous medication, my mom asked the nurse what I was being given. The nurse replied that I was given what Dr. G. ordered.

Please Visit www.LifeTeamStrategy.com

Before we left Indiana, the nurse gave my mother a stack of papers for both her and Dr. G. with strict instructions for my care. In that paperwork, which my mother always brought with her to the hospital, was a list of medications I was not to be given because of the negative side effects they would have with my chemotherapy drugs. My mother checked the labels on the bags that were being infused at that time. Sure enough, I was currently being administered a drug that was on that list. My mother quickly ran to the nurse and showed her the list explaining to her what it all meant and frantically asked her to stop the drug. The nurse stated that she didn't have the authority to do that. My mom asked her to call the doctor and tell him what was happening. "Well, we can't question the doctor" was the reply. That nurse could have won "**Shover** of the Month" for that one.

My mother repeated that the treatment I was being given was under the direction of the doctors in Indiana and that this new doctor wasn't familiar with it. When the nurse turned a deaf ear, my mother commandeered the use of a hospital phone and called Indiana. She was able to reach the nurse who gave us the paperwork, and when my mother told her what was going on, the nurse shouted, "WHAT?" and asked to talk to my nurse. After tearing the nurse a new asshole for a few minutes in true **Starter** fashion for not listening to my mother or trying to contact the doctor, she ordered her to, "Pull the medication now."

My mother was able to get back on the phone and talk to the nurse in Indiana one last time while the unconcerned nurse removed the medication. She told my mom that she would personally call Dr. G. so that this doesn't happen again. My mother and the new nurse proceeded to take the thick blankets off of me as they were clearly useless against the chemical chills induced by this medical faux pas. The chills soon subsided, and I was left in great pain and completely exhausted. The episode had lasted about an hour before the medication was finally stopped. I was left trying to catch my breath and feeling like I'd been run over by every car of a mile-long freight train. I was furious as I saw myself become a victim of my circumstances and what appeared to be an indifferent medical staff of **Shovers**.

My mother tried to arrange for a hospital social worker to come and see me but was told the hospital was undergoing a reorganization period and one wasn't available. So I was left with no one to help me deal with my anger and fears. As far as I know, Dr. G. never commented on this incident to my mother, and he certainly never apologized to me. This demonstrated **Shover**-like aloofness on his part, which I would eventually discover was indicative of his bedside manner.

I became so defiant that week that at one point I grabbed a large piece of modeling clay my mother had brought me to help relieve stress and fashioned it into a five fingered hand. Four of the fingers of this hand were clenched into a fist while the middle finger was extended. Not long after I'd made my bird statue, one of the nurses walked in and had a hearty laugh over it. Then she said, "When I come to work tomorrow I'll have something for you." What she brought me was a gag gift she'd received in college. It was a small rubber stamp of none other than a five fingered fist with the middle finger extended. She was also kind enough to supply me with a bright red ink pad. I expressed my extreme gratitude for her gift and then generously inked the rubber stamp and placed it right in the middle of my forehead. I wanted to be sure that anyone who entered my room knew exactly how I was feeling.

I finished that round of chemo the next day and left for home, still exhausted from what had happened. As soon as I got out of the car and started walking toward the house, a giant wave of nausea hit me, and I stumbled into the bushes in front of the house to puke my guts out. I felt my mother gently place her hand on my back as she asked if I was all right. "I just have to lie down," I said.

I Reach Out for Support

A few days later I began making phone calls to my school friends to finally tell them what was happening and to reach out to them for support. I had made many friends through a Christian youth group before I'd graduated and thought if I could count on anyone, it would be them. We were always saying how we would be there for each other. I quickly got the impression that the "always" had conditions. After I told them what was happening, they expressed concern, and a few even came to see me over the next week, saying they'd pray for me. Then they disappeared. They had gone from being **Starters** to **Sitters**.

When I would phone any of them, I would always get the same responses: "I'm too busy to talk now," "I'm just on my way out" or "I have someone over now—can I call you back?" They never did. I couldn't understand why they behaved this way. The prayer was nice, but what I really needed was them. Aside from my family, who was already strained by all of this, these were the only people I had to turn to. No one could offer me an explanation for why my loyalty as a friend was being rewarded in this way. I began to feel abandoned and alone. My anger began to turn to rage as I focused on the sense of betrayal I felt. Those around me quickly began to see this. I was becoming more frightened and defensive and in my mind began looking around for whoever was going to hurt me next.

Please Visit www.LifeTeamStrategy.com

After that week of chemo was over, I brought my anger home, and no one in my house was safe from it. I started turning into a real **Shouter**. The simple question of how was I feeling was no longer a matter of concern but a condescending remark in my mind, one which guaranteed the asker a "How do you think I feel?" tongue-lashing.

I was so hurt by the desertion of the friends I'd cared so much about that I was afraid any sign of concern might be false and conditional. My family was also becoming more and more unsupportive as they grew more overwhelmed themselves. With the exception of my mother, my father and siblings became **Sitters** if for no other reason than they just didn't have anything left to give. I was not raised in a home where problems were met head-on anyway. The ostrich mentality of stick your head in the sand and wait for the problem to go away or say something so mean that the other person gets too angry to continue the conversation was the prevailing strategy.

Chris and Melissa also took turns screaming at me as they began to see me as a **Shover** who was dominating our mother's attention. In spite of my best efforts they didn't realize that mom's attention had more to do with the circumstances than a preference of me over them. They had every reason to have hurt feelings during this time, but they didn't seem to realize that if I could have changed things, I would have. They were clearly at a loss for how to deal with my illness. My dad found escape in his work, and my siblings began spending more and more time with their friends. I understand that this was probably good for them because it helped them maintain normalcy in their own lives. My mom tried her best to be there for me, but she had a whole family to take care of and a business to run, so even she had her limits. Everyone had their limits, and my dear girlfriend "J" was about to reach hers.

THE DOWNWARD SPIRAL

I had been throwing my anger around incessantly, and "J" had been able to remain loyal and patient throughout much of the **Shout**ing I was doing. She would walk to the hospital every day, which was a short distance from her house, and sit with me for hours. Sometimes she would even fall asleep in the chair. Unfortunately, her family wasn't much different from mine when it came to problem solving, so she was left without anyone to talk to at home. While I valued her support, I was overpowered by the fear that I would lose it, as I had lost everyone else's. The anger brought about by this fear is what I believe to be the

Please Visit www.LifeTeamStrategy.com

main cause of what happened next. I would call her at home, but she wouldn't stay on the phone long. I sensed she was purposely distancing herself from me. After about a week of this, I confronted her with my belief that she was avoiding me, and she laid into me with horribly, cutting words. The one statement in her barrage of anger that stands out the most in my mind is when she said, "I never loved you. I was infatuated. Now get over it, and get on with your life."

I was devastated. I tried mailing her some letters, but there was no response. At the time all I could see was the increased anger and betrayal I was feeling. In my mind I had truly lost everything. The support of my friends, the love of a wonderful girl and a promising future had been ripped away. It appeared that all of the guarantees I'd been given in the relationships in my life were lies—conditional truths and rules that could be changed at the whim of the participants. I was enraged at myself for having been so blind and so vulnerable. I felt physically hideous and foolish for having trusted others. This rage gradually turned into depression and despair as I dwelled on what I saw as a hopeless situation. I felt Totally Screwed. I concluded that the world was a horrible place that had turned its back on me.

As I sat in the hospital, those feelings kept building until I thought I would burst. I wouldn't discuss them openly because I felt I couldn't trust anyone. But I had to get them out somehow. I'd always found writing, especially poetry, to be therapeutic as well as a safe way to express my feelings. I could be honest without the risk of criticism. Luckily, there was a pad of paper and a pen in the nightstand drawer next to my hospital bed. I picked them up and began writing. At first all I did was write lines of profanity to try and get my anger out. Then I would crumple up the paper and throw it away, hoping my anger would go with it. But that didn't work. I decided to write about my actual feelings to clear my head a little. I wrote about how miserable I was feeling in the following poem.

> I wander blindly through the snow,
> I wander without thought.
> My skin is cold, my eyes are dry,
> My spirit is distraught.
>
> The sky is of the darkest gray
> Without a hint of light.
> My eyes long for the light of day
> But only see the night.

I stagger forward for an end
To a journey all uphill.
The only progress ever made
Is that of standing still.

My heart was once a place of warmth
Where only love could reign.
But now it's cold and motionless
And now knows only pain.

With the shrill and force of the freezing wind
My shrinking soul grows colder.
What used to be my fire for life
Is reduced down to a smolder.

It's as though I'm in the deepest chasm
With a wall of ice throughout.
And I can only stand in desperate silence
With no hope of getting out.

I face the wind with desperation
My face without expression.
The only companion I possess
Is that of deep depression.

I stand in total misery
As I breathe a freezing breath.
I realize one absolute,
We all face certain death.

I had become a world-class **Shouter** at my own expense. At the time it didn't seem there was a life left for me. I was consumed only by the life I'd lost. There were some around me who made an effort to comfort me, but at that point I was no longer willing to listen. I had shrunk into a cocoon of self-pity and doubt. My head began racing with thoughts of "Why me?" "What the hell did I do to deserve this?" "How dare they do this to me?" "Why do I bother living?" "Why can't I just die?" I was sliding deeper and deeper into depression. As if the previous poem wasn't deep enough.

Although I was told that week of chemo would be my last, I found no comfort in it, as I had given up on life. I had realized that all of the lessons and truths that I had clung to were not the absolutes I'd been encouraged to see them as. I'd

Please Visit www.LifeTeamStrategy.com

always thought that if I lead a good life, nothing bad would ever happen to me and that if I were there for others, they'd be there for me. Nothing I had ever learned in church or at school could ever have prepared me for this.

I was becoming suicidal, and this was the most terrifying feeling I'd ever known. I couldn't trust how I saw others and wasn't sure who I was anymore, so I essentially lost faith in myself. I was lost. I sat alone in my hospital bed and at the very moment I needed someone the most, Laura walked in. She simply asked how I was doing, and I burst into tears. She sat on the side of my bed and held my hand while I cried. "What's wrong?" she asked. "Everything's wrong" I answered. "Everything. Why me? Why did this have to happen to me? I don't know what to do."

She looked at me with compassion in her eyes, but behind her compassion, I could tell she was feeling helpless in that moment. Although all she could say is that things will get better, her being there when I needed someone, if only for a few minutes, was a tremendous gift. She demonstrated that it's possible to be a **Starter** simply by being there.

When I was finally able to go home, I locked myself in my room and pulled all the shades. I spent the next week crying and sometimes yelling. My parents were frightened because they didn't know what to do for me. In my mind I kept rehashing all that had happened. Soon, throwing fits grew old as all the yelling was making me hoarse. I got so enraged at one moment that I punched a hole in my bedroom wall. When I later looked in the hole I noticed that my hand had barely passed between two boards. Had I been even a little off, I probably would have broken my hand.

I realized that I was clearly out of control and sat down trying to catch my breath and regain some composure. I saw one of my old notebooks across the room and decided to focus my energies again on writing what I was feeling. So I picked up my pen and began writing about the sense of betrayal I was feeling.

> *My doctor said it was cancer. He thought he got it all, but he didn't. Then the cancer came back. He told me these treatments would make it better, but things got worse. I turned to my friends for support. I had stood by them after all. But they turned their backs on me. They treated me like a ghost—like I was already a name on a tombstone. As the treatment increased, so did my pain and my tears.*

I had contemplated suicide several times throughout my ordeal but never once tried it. There was a little **Starter** left in the back of my mind that kept saying don't do it. Just wait one more day. Maybe it will change. Nothing on the surface was changing, but still, something was holding me up. What made me want to give up? What made me want to stay?

At some point I began stubbornly refusing to let what was happening to me ruin my life. I was tired of feeling this way, and no one around me seemed to have any answers. I was not going to allow all of the negativity of the situation beat me. I was tired of not having any control. It was time to start asking myself some serious questions. Again, I wrote it all out.

> *Is my life worth living? Does my life have a meaning? Is my being here significant or just a brief flicker in the sky? Is life about all the material things? If so, life can be taken away from me. If life is about the things we can all enjoy, then life won't ever go away. I need life to be about the things that don't wear out, that are timeless and have endurance. Before now I valued the temporary things and was let down hard. At this moment I ask myself, what am I living for? Is being alive itself the greatest gift? Are material things required to make it worth living? Right now it seems life is all I have. I have to start somewhere. I'm still uncertain as to why I should stay. But there is no denying, for some reason, I chose to stay today.*

In spite of the fact I'd immersed myself in hopelessness, it became evident that something was going to have to give. I realized that the question "Why me?" could not be answered.

2

From Suffering to Living

"Why me?" was irrelevant. The fact of the matter was that it *was* me. So the real question was "Where do I go from here?" Over the next week I spent enough time in solitude with my feelings of depression to realize they were getting me nowhere. I discovered that the cancer of depression was overtaking me and becoming a bigger problem than the physical one. I began getting sick of feeling miserable. I was 18 years old, and if I was going to live, I wasn't about to spend the rest of my life living under a cloud. I decided that I'd had enough and was going to find a way to do things differently. I had decided to become a **Starter** again but was unsure how or where to begin. I knew I wanted out of this downward spiral, but my fears of further disappointment and my doubts about life in general left me without a place to begin. This is a classic case of **Shoving:** I knew I wanted things to get better, but my doubt was holding me back.

THE FIRST STEP TOWARD HEALING

One day I was sitting in my room, and out of boredom and curiosity, I glanced at my bookshelf where a lot of old books had found their way to collect dust. I noticed a particular book with a Chinese author named Lao Tzu; the book was called *Tao Te Ching*. I read the back cover, which said the passages in this book were written a few thousand years ago. As I looked through its pages, I found that although the text was written for a time long past, its words slapped me in the face with a stinging relevance. I didn't read the book cover to cover at first but leafed through its pages. One passage in particular was the catalyst I needed to move me in a new direction, and it will forever stick in my mind. It said "The journey of a thousand miles begins with a single step." After reading this my mind began to calm, if only for a moment. I had just found a **Starter** from 2,000 years ago that was helping me now because he took the time to write his thoughts down. Through his thoughts the magnitude of my circumstances had just been simplified. All I needed to do was start where I was—to take a single step to begin my long journey out of these circumstances. It wasn't a matter of solving everything at once but instead just one step at a time. I was still at a loss for what that step was, however. As I read more, it was as if this book had been written for me.

Tao Te Ching stated that the source of all things gives birth to both good and evil without taking sides. It welcomes both entities as complementary forces in life. It then asks the following questions: Can you let yourself become as a child? Can you love others without imposing your will? Can you deal with things by letting them take their course? Can you have without wanting to possess? Can you act without expectation and without desire to control? For this is the way of peace and virtue. I had found the key to my journey back. Amazing how the first **Starter** on my way back from depression would be a man I would never physically meet.

These few passages seemed to answer my most biting questions. I found it particularly interesting that I found the answers right when I began looking for them. As soon as I changed my question from "why was I so depressed?" to "how can I be happy again?" the answers changed. Until now I was consumed by the belief that others were supposed to give me what I wanted from them and were responsible for meeting my expectations. I had been fighting the whole process and trying to keep my life as it had been, failing to allow it to take its own course. I discovered that starting over meant not having back what I had lost—an important lesson considering there was no way I could get back what the cancer had already taken from me. I had to learn to deal with the change that was rapidly present in my life and learn how to use it to my advantage instead of fearing and resenting it. Of course, the book made it all sound so simple. But how was I supposed to learn to implement this in my life? I was frightened before when faced with the loss of a belief system that had suddenly become inapplicable to my life. Even more frightening now was the thought of learning to trust a new one.

THE HARA DECISION

I had to take an important step. I had to put it all on the line and reach down into my gut to find out if this was the right direction for me to go. This step is a powerful first step in curing the fear that compels you to hang on to the security of your old ways of thinking. As I mentioned, the time came when I knew I had to radically change my way of thinking, and it was at that moment that I made what I now call a "Hara decision." Let me first differentiate between other types of decisions.

A decision made with your mind is strong but often lacks the rigor to hold up against mental fatigue, frustration, confusion, the influence of others or simple everyday distractions. Many of us take our cues and are guided by forces outside of ourselves, which leaves room for the introduction of doubt from the **Shouters** in life. As such, a person looking for direction outside of oneself is less likely to stick with a decision very long when his or her environment resists his or her efforts.

A heartfelt decision causes you to lead with emotions and is often impulsive, which can leave you open to pain, suffering and eventually defeat. Guided by good intentions, you're again open to influence from the **Shouters** and often stop when your intentions are rebuked and your feelings get hurt.

A Hara decision is made with the conviction and motivation of a **Starter** and is the most powerful decision you can make. This kind of decision is one that rises from the very core of your being. Most people understand it as our "gut feeling," or instinct. In Japanese medicine as well as in many martial arts systems, the Hara is the area three inches below your navel and as many inches inward. It is the center of your body—your center of gravity as well as the center of your spirit. While you walk down the street, it is your Hara that keeps you physically balanced, upright and steady. The direction your Hara points is the direction you're walking in. As such it guides you in all matters. It is easier to push someone off balance when they are bent over because their Hara is pointing toward the ground. When pushed, their Hara leads them in the direction it is pointing.

When something feels dangerous and you get an uneasy feeling in your gut, that is your Hara talking. Your spiritual center tells you when something threatens your balance physically, mentally and spiritually. But most important, it tells you when something feels right and is the right thing to do. It is an intrinsic and ancient compass that life gives us for our own protection and guidance. If you follow the guidance of your Hara and trust that "gut feeling" from the center of who you are, you will feel more confident in your decisions. This ability to work from the gut is a key characteristic of **Starters**.

When your decisions come from your Hara, they will always stem from who you are. They become a part of you and an expression of your inner wisdom that knows the direction you need to be going. Once you have made a Hara decision to pursue something, accomplishing it becomes as important to you as breathing. Your guidance is not derived solely from external cues or by impulse. Instead, you are driven by an internal well of commitment and passion that is the source of what defines you. I was so desperate for answers and change that my commitment for something better was as strong as the commitment someone might have in trying to escape a burning house. As such, a Hara decision is so powerful and focused that it has no doubt.

    I had made the Hara decision that life as I currently knew it was unacceptable, and I was going to make it into what I wanted it to be. I was going to find control again where I could. I was going to be in charge of my life and my future. Hopelessness wasn't acceptable, and I wouldn't stop until I had the best life I could make for myself. I pointed my Hara, my whole being, in the direction of my goal, and, therefore, I would only stop doing what was best for me when my life stops. This decision was the most powerful step in beginning the process of getting out of my own way.

ISOLATION

Over the next week I studied *Tao Te Ching* in greater depth and began gaining a little more enthusiasm about a positive future. As my mental resolve strengthened, I felt my physical health begin to slowly deteriorate even more. I was starting to get very sick, unlike anything I'd experienced up to this point. A high fever, a burning sore throat and a stomachache quickly developed. My complexion became pale white. My mother had observed this progression as well, but we hoped these were only side effects of the chemotherapy and would soon pass. Quietly I feared my cancer had become more aggressive. Toward the end of the week, I was bedridden. I was coughing and my throat was so sore that I couldn't eat anything or even swallow my own saliva. Speaking was difficult, and I felt pain in every inch of my body. Finding a comfortable position was absolutely impossible. I felt like I was going to die.

    My mother called Dr. G. to tell him what was happening and asked if she should take me to the hospital. He thought there was a chance that my white blood cell count had dropped due to the chemotherapy, which would leave me unable to fight off infection. He discounted this possibility, however, because his experience told him that if this were going to happen, it would have happened long before. He was the expert, so my mother sat with me for the next couple of hours, doing her best to keep me comfortable and ride this out. By then I had had enough and told my mom to take me to the hospital. I didn't care what the doctor said; I only knew how I felt. My mom and my sister helped me to the car and drove me to the emergency room.

I waited for over an hour in the waiting room, where I almost fainted twice. My mom repeatedly went to the reception desk and begged to have me seen more quickly but to no avail. While I sat there trying to muster up some strength, I had an experience that brought a huge smile to my face and also shed some light on things. Sitting in the chairs across from me was a Hispanic man and his son, who couldn't have been more than three years old. They where waiting for the boy's mother, who I discovered later had come in to have an injury to her arm looked at. The little boy was fascinated by my appearance. Here I sat as pale as glue with practically no body hair to speak of. The boy stared at me awestruck like he was seeing a ghost, which wasn't too far off. He looked me right in the face and pointed at me with one hand as he touched his own head with the other, saying to his father with amazement, "No pelo. No pelo," which means "No hair. No hair."

His father tried to quiet him, but I could only smile and gesture to his father that it was quite all right. My mother had overheard this and understood enough Spanish to know what the boy was saying and to explain to his father why I looked this way. The father gave me a smile of encouragement as he talked with his boy. By the time the boy's mother returned, it was finally my turn to be seen.

I was taken back and laid on a cart where the E.R. doctor came over to me and introduced herself. My mother gave her my medical history, which was written all over me by then. In spite of what my doctor had said, she told us she would order a blood test in order to get my white cell count. About half an hour later the doctor came back with the results and said that I would be staying. She explained that I had a condition called neutropenia, which is "doctor talk" for a low white blood cell count.

My white count had not only dropped; it had dropped a lot. Where the normal count was about 4,000, mine had dropped to 700. With so little immunity to fight with, I had contracted a systemic infection that caused both my esophagus and my stomach to become inflamed. I hadn't eaten in several days because swallowing had been too painful, so to remedy the pain the doctor mixed up a cocktail of antacid and an anesthetic called xylocaine for me to drink. It was like trying to swallow toothpaste, and its affects wore off about 15 minutes after I swallowed it. Then I had to wait another hour for an isolation room to be sterilized before I was admitted to the hospital. In all Dr. G had acted like a **Shover** in this instance as he arrogantly assumed that the course of my health wouldn't deviate from his past experience. As a result, instead of advising a trip to the hospital he told me to stay put, which was clearly not in my best interest.

Please Visit www.LifeTeamStrategy.com

It was about one in the morning when I was finally taken to my room. My mother left with plans to return first thing in the morning. A nurse got me settled in bed and then left the room. Physically I was the worst I had ever been. I felt like I had been dropped from an airplane without a parachute. A few minutes later my stomach had decided that it didn't like the E.R. doctor's xylocaine cocktail. I quickly grabbed a basin from my bedside table, which was luckily within reach, and proceeded to throw up for the next ten minutes. I barely had time to inhale before I would vomit again. It hurt so badly that it felt like I was throwing up razor blades. My throat might as well have been torn out of my body. It took me a while to catch my breath, after which I collapsed asleep from exhaustion. It seems that a lot of my rest during these months was gained only at the hands of exhaustion.

The next morning around five or six I was rudely awaken. I felt someone nudging my shoulder and heard a male voice saying, "Hey, wake up." It was Dr. G—the expert **Shover** whose bedside manner left a lot to be desired. His attitude was pretty cancerous at that moment. All I could do was look at him and wish I had the strength to punch him out. This was the second time his expertise had made my suffering worse. The first time by having a drug administered to me that he had been instructed not to give me under any circumstances. He looked at my test results and said, "It looks like your white cells took a nosedive."

He didn't apologize for making a mistake; he didn't admit he was wrong for telling my mother there was no way that this was the problem. Perhaps his ego couldn't handle the idea that he was human. I would have respected him greatly had he admitted his error; instead, I resented him. All he did was tell me that I would be staying there while intravenous antibiotics were pumped into me to fight off the infection. This would give my white blood cells a chance to replenish themselves. Until my count was high enough to provide me with sufficient immunity, I would have to stay isolated.

I had been placed in reverse isolation, which meant I was in a sterile room by myself where I would be protected from everyone else who might have germs. Everyone had to scrub their arms up to the elbow and wear a mask a gown and surgical gloves if they wanted to enter my room. This was difficult to endure. I was denied human contact except through sterile rubber gloves and masks, and that contact was usually from nurses or someone who woke me up to poke me with a needle. My mother couldn't even give me a hug.

Every morning at five someone came into my room to draw blood so they could check my white cell count and see how I was doing. At this point I had only one good vein left in my right arm to draw blood from. Throughout my various hospital stays, my IVs had been started and restarted so many times that by the end of my chemotherapy experience, every major vein in both of my forearms and hands were scorching hot with inflammation, a condition called phlebitis. The veins on the top, bottom and sides of both arms were so swollen that they stuck out like the veins on a bodybuilder's arm. But mine were red, swollen and too painful to even touch. The one remaining vein that was being used to draw blood from had been poked so many times that you could actually see a circle of holes that weren't being given a chance to heal. Between my phlebitis and puncture holes, I looked like a heroin junkie.

I felt and looked like garbage and was in so much pain that even the weight of my blankets was sometimes too much to bear. The antibiotics slowly seemed to start working, and my white count slowly climbed back to a healthy level. Although this physical isolation made me feel even more emotionally isolated, being alone was the very catalyst I needed to take that first step on my thousand-mile journey.

THE LESSON OF THE CLOCK

As I had committed myself to finding control where I could, my mind was focused on any opportunity to learn something new that I could use to speed me on my way. Toward the middle of the week, the isolation was really getting to me. It was so quiet I could hear the ticking of the clock that hung on the wall directly across from me. Its face appeared to be staring me down. I began to study it, tick-tock, tick-tock. I then looked out my window and saw cars driving by. I heard a train roll by and saw airplanes overhead. Time was moving on, going forward, tick-tock, tick-tock. Time wouldn't stop. The world was going on without me. If I were to die the world would be just fine. The world wouldn't stop just because I did. The hands of the clock would continue to turn, and the world would keep on turning. This was an incredibly humbling realization.

When the only activity available to me was to watch time pass, it was easy to see it happening without me. Amazing how an everyday object like a clock can be such a valuable learning tool—a real **Starter** if you ask me. From then on I began looking at everyday experiences differently. I figured if a clock could teach me so much, what else was out there waiting for me? After the lesson of the clock, I could no longer maintain a sense of self-importance. I could no longer justify the idea that my expectations ought to have been met by those I felt betrayed me. I now knew that I wasn't so important that I couldn't be done without. I realized that my friends quite possibly chose to do without me instead of dealing with my circumstances and me. I was still upset about it, but it was beginning to make sense. I could no longer sit around expecting people to be **Starters** just because I wanted them to be.

A few weeks earlier I had come to the conclusion that something was going to have to give. I just realized that something was me—I was going to have to be my own **Starter** and give to myself. I was going to have to be responsible for finding within myself, the support I needed to get through this.

Along with an increase in white blood cells, my various blood tests revealed that my cancer was gone. I was in remission, which meant there was no sign of cancer anywhere in my body. With the news that I was going to live finally confirmed, I realized more than ever that I would have to get with the program and learn how to live all over again.

For once in a long time I began to feel in charge again. No longer was there anyone or anything to blame for how I was feeling. I decided I would take responsibility for that. Where everything else in my life had fallen short, I was going to have to rise to the occasion to make sure everything would turn out the best it could. A lot had happened that I couldn't change, I was no longer viewing these things as obstacles but instead as building blocks. I figured, so what if life had thrown me a pile of horse crap? I was going to do what was necessary to turn the crap into fertilizer and grow a beautiful garden.

With this new resolve of spirit and will, I had made an additional Hara decision that would shape the rest of my life. From now on the story of my life would change from victim to victor. Victimization was the role I'd played since this whole thing began, and that didn't get me anywhere. I was no longer going to allow others to decide how I felt about myself or allow circumstances to be bigger than me. I would no longer let life happen *to* me. I was going to start happening to it, in the best way I knew how.

As I lay in my hospital bed, basking in my new resolve, I closed my eyes and tried to rest a little. I began taking some slow, deep breaths. I did so in an attempt to relax and alleviate some of the physical pain I was feeling and hopefully to take my mind off of it for a while. The room was very silent, and all I could hear was the clock. As I started to relax more, my breathing became less deliberate and took over for itself. I just lay there and paid attention to my breathing as my chest rose and fell. I began relaxing deeper and deeper and felt the preoccupation with my pain diminish as I found comfort in the depth of my breath. I found to some degree that I was actually able to relax my pain away.

Please Visit www.LifeTeamStrategy.com

As I felt my breathing change, I remembered what *Tao Te Ching* had said about how life was in a state of perpetual change. I could hear the clock ticking as I felt the rising and falling of my chest. This constant changing of my breath was the changing of life; it was this change that was sustaining my life. As time changed and passed, so did my breath and so did my life. I began seeing that as I had been resisting change, I was actually resisting life, because change was the force that was sustaining my life at this very moment. As my chest rose and fell, as my heart beat in my chest, so did the rhythm of life.

I started thinking about all of the loss I'd endured and the pain I'd experienced, as well as all of the things in the future that I feared I would never have. I never thought for a moment that everything I needed depended on what was happening right now, this moment. I was alive because of the present changing of my breath and the beating of my heart. I didn't need to worry about the past, because it had changed and become the present. The future isn't even here yet, so what in the world can I do about that? I had enough to worry about in the present. My own breath had shown me where I was at in life and who I was. I am here, I am now, and this is where I must begin my journey. I opened my eyes and sat up. I started contemplating all of those everyday things I hadn't given proper attention to because of my preoccupations with the befores and afters of my life. I then reached over to the nightstand, grabbed my pad of paper and began writing.

I look around this very moment. What do I see? I see the brightness of the sunshine, clouds passing overhead, my reflection in the window. What do I hear? I hear the joyful singing of a bird, a plane flying overhead, people talking and laughing outside my room. The wind rustling through the trees, the sound of my own heartbeat, the calm of my own breath.

Where am I right now, this very moment? Where is all of this taking place? I am in the present, nowhere else. The seeds of my past have blossomed into where I am now. But I cannot climb back into a seed; I must either continue to grow or give up and die. I must give in or win. Complacency is the enemy of growth. So growth is my choice.

I have been hanging on to the anger and sadness of the past. Hindering my own growth in the present. Longing for the pleasures of the past as well as clinging to its sorrows. Never once trying to do anything now.

From this moment on I will make a commitment to myself. Once the present moment passes, it becomes the past, so I will let it go. This is an essential rule of life that I've missed until now. Now I will embody it as one of my greatest assets, so I will not be distracted from the life in front of me. I promise to let the moment pass, and any anger, fear and sadness that came with it. These feelings may have been relevant in that moment, but the moment is gone. Why keep these feelings now? I

Please Visit www.LifeTeamStrategy.com

will never again stand in the way of my own experience of the full joy and happiness of life. For how can I enjoy life, if I am never here?

This was an incredible revelation that was amazingly therapeutic to write. If I was going to achieve my goal of a better life, I had to be constantly aware of what the current situation provided for me. Imagine that—the present moment was and is a **Starter**. I had to keep my eye out for the clock and any other resource I could tap into on my journey. I believe that if my life hadn't unfolded in this way, I may not have achieved this realization. Having lost confidence in my past and approaching an uncertain future, the present was all I had left. I learned that I can always count on the present, because it will always be here with plenty of opportunities. Although I had wanted to be free of this depression for so long, it seemed to be leaving a little more quickly than I thought it would. As such I chose simply to enjoy the experience.

THE BENDING OF THE TREE

I turned and looked out my window beyond the road and into the forest preserve that was carpeted with trees. I suddenly recalled what I had read about not trying to control change but allowing it to take its course. So I closely observed how the trees kept adjusting to the breeze, back and forth, back and forth. I was struck by the spontaneity and resilience of the branches as they gently swayed. I realized that the trees were living in the present moment as they embraced and adjusted to the changing breeze. The trees were examples of natural **Starters**.

In these few moments I learned how I needed to deal with the adversity I was faced with. For so long my coping skills were tainted by overreacting to the present, anticipating the future and clinging to the past—the very skills the tree eloquently did without. Instead, the tree bent only as much as necessary; it didn't resist the oncoming breeze and didn't stay bent in anticipation that the wind might blow again. The tree dealt only with what needed to be dealt with as it arose. As I watched the tree, to me it became even clearer how being concerned with past losses and future gains was irrelevant in dealing with the present. Although the past often plays a role in most people's lives, it is how we adjust to it in the present that is the key.

For the next few days I sat on this discovery and let it take root. I kept watching the trees and relaxing with my breath. I now realized more than ever that the solutions I needed were all around me, right outside my window. The challenges

I was facing were life challenges more than they were human challenges. Other living things were and are dealing with the same struggles I was; I need only look to them for solutions. All this time I was surrounded by **Starters**, right outside my window.

After seven days in isolation, I was able to convince Dr. G. to let me go home. My white cell count was only a little over 1,000, but the doctor was willing to let me go because I was feeling better and agreed to take special precautions to help prevent against getting sick again. I left the hospital with the first smile anyone had seen on my face in months.

Over the next couple of days at home, I stayed inside and read what I had written over the past week. I was amazed how through a simple process in nature, I was beginning to unlearn the expectations of my past that had tainted my ability to deal with the present. It was becoming obvious that I needed to begin looking at my expectations more closely, as they were responsible for so much of the emotional suffering I had endured.

Although thinking this through helped me realize what I had been doing to myself, it would not be an easy task to incorporate all of this into my thinking. My emotions were still pretty raw, and I was still reactionary in many ways. But I had made my decision, and there was no turning back. Having all of this free time to invest in deep reflection obviously helped to reinforce the path I was now on. I was feeling much better physically, emotionally and mentally. I was well on my way. It was amazing how a little hope fueled by an unbreakable commitment can speed your recovery.

I was slowly regaining my strength as my infection disappeared, but I was facing a new experience that sapped my strength. I had held so much anger inside for so many months that I was wiped out after discovering it was safe to let it go. It seemed that carrying emotional burdens was more tiring than toting physical ones. With no one to blame any longer, there was nothing left to fuel such negativity. It just sort of burned out like a fire that had been robbed of oxygen.

I looked out the living room window and saw a gorgeous day waiting outside. The sky was clear blue, and as I stuck my head out the back door I felt the nice warm air against my face. I couldn't stay in on a day like this, so I grabbed my pad of paper and walked outside to my backyard. I sat a lawn chair in the middle of the yard and took a seat. I simply sat there taking in everything to see what I could discover. Did I ever discover.

So much of what I had thought about life was determined by the conclusions I'd drawn from what I had seen and heard and felt. I believed the obvious to be true. Now I looked around more closely at all of nature's colors. I listened. The wind and the trees were rustling. The birds were chirping. The grass had never looked greener or smelled so sweet. I decided to look within my senses to explore what they were telling me and to see if I was hearing, seeing and sensing all that I could. If I weren't, then how could I go about removing the blinders that had led to my misperceptions in the first place?

I was reaching a place where I felt I could learn to trust again now that I was discovering just how different life could be. I was finding life to be more tolerant and forgiving than I had been. I was learning to be more alive. As I learned, I also wrote.

> *I used to only look with my eyes, which made it difficult to see. Perhaps if I look a little longer, a little deeper, I might find the truth underneath. It is so easy to become distracted by the colors or the shapes and forget to look beyond them. It's important to note the labels I use and the values I place. How much of my life is not a result of how things are but more what I do with how things are?*
>
> *It's beginning to look like things are at their best before I smear my impressions all over them. From now on it's experience first, interpretation second. My ears need to listen more closely, more thoroughly. Then maybe I'll truly hear. I'll look beyond the noise, listening for what's being said instead of for what I want to hear. Then my life will continue to improve, as the accuracy of what I'm taking in increases.*

For too long I had been blinded by superficiality—taking things for how they appeared and failing to look more deeply. It was amazing how much more there was to be experienced when I wasn't hastily assembling things according to my preferences and personal judgments. My experience with cancer taught me that things in life occur in one of two ways: They happen either how I intend them to happen or how they actually happen. My preferences and expectations had nothing to do with whether I got cancer or not. Of course, I would have preferred not to have suffered this way. But preferences aside, what actually happened is what I was left to deal with. As I began studying my experiences, I was becoming more aware of what was actually happening before me. I realized that I needed to stop seeing what I liked and didn't like or how I could make a situation go in my favor. Instead of only looking for what I wanted, I could just pay attention to the things around me. I would soon discover the things I never even knew I needed. Had I not been paying attention, I may have missed them.

THE LESSON OF THE LEAF

My mind was spinning with all this new information. Life may be capable of going on without me, but since I would not be leaving anytime soon, I hoped, I needed to find a way to jump back into the life stream.

As I sat in the yard trying to figure out just where I fit into the scheme of things, my eyes began to wander around the yard. I noticed the leaves on the trees rustling in the breeze, and my attention was soon drawn to a single leaf hanging from a branch overhead. I watched it as it danced around, with the sunlight flickering through. It was at that moment that it hit me. I remembered what I had learned in school about how the sun works with the trees to create the oxygen in the air I was breathing at that moment. In addition to the sunlight, the tree uses the carbon dioxide exhaled by living, breathing things like myself. All this time I held the knowledge of the power of interdependence in my head, but it wasn't until right then that I truly felt I was part of it and understood the significance of what that meant. I just realized how important I was in the scheme of things, in the process of life.

The more I thought about it the more I realized how as I sat there, I was an active part of the symphony of life being played in this moment. The leaf and I couldn't survive without each other, and neither of us could exist without the sun. When I looked at a leaf or even myself, I realized that I was looking at a reflection of everything else.

I'd never felt so insignificant and yet so essential in my whole life. I had to give my mind a breather as I was getting a little ahead of myself, and I realized my body needed a breather as well. I was still feeling a little weak and decided to go inside the house to take a nap. Even sitting outside in the heat was enough to exhaust me. When I awoke, I got something to eat and started again. I felt a little **Shouting** going on and some trembling in my gut as I contemplated giving up the old ideas I'd been clinging to for so long. My Hara was in the process of a major change in direction. In spite of my nervousness, the excitement I was feeling from all of these new life-affirming discoveries made any fears pale by comparison. My commitment was bigger than my fears. I began to remember what I had read in *Tao Te Ching* and started again to ask myself those very important questions.

A Child's Eyes

Could I let myself become like a child? After having been through so much could I learn to see everything for the first time again? I was in the unique position of having to literally start over. I was more or less a beginner.

I remembered the little boy I encountered in the waiting room who was in awe of my baldness. He was a child learning about life. I watched my young niece Jessica playing; she was so full of enthusiasm and possibilities. How could I once again become this way? How could I proceed without presumption? I looked inside myself to discover just what it meant to me to be a child again, a beginner. I quietly began writing.

> *The eyes of a child are those of a beginner, bright and awake. Every experience is a new one. A child's eyes are like a mirror. When something is held up to it you see an exact reflection of what it sees. The mirror does not try to change it to suit itself. Neither does the child's eyes; they just accept it. In a child's eyes all things are equal and all things are special because all things are new. They are life, they are to cherish, and a child does"*
>
> Many minds experience the changing reality before them. Then suddenly, they get in the way of their own experiences. They grab hold of that moment and freeze it within a thought. Content that this is it, they stop watching.
>
> A child awakens each morning, bright eyed and eager to take on the unlimited possibilities before it. It knows no limitations. Every day is truly new, no habit or daily grind. If something is new, keep it new; when you keep it new it never gets old. When something gets old it eventually dies. See through child's eyes, the newness of this moment and keep life alive. Just watch, experience, live, as a child.
>
> The eyes of a child don't doubt that which is before them, they watch, they trust. These eyes don't fear, they have courage and take risks. The eyes of a child are as full of beauty and wonder as the life in which they actively participate. The eyes of a child are those of a beginner. As the sunrise begins a new day, as each turning of the clock begins 24 crisp new hours of life. As each rising and falling of our own breath provides us with the beginning of one more moment of life. Watch the children. Watch their eyes, watch life unfold through a beginners eyes.

I Shall Be the Sun

I can be no more prejudiced of another person than I can be of myself. We are simply waves flowing side by side, all part of the same ocean with the appearance of being separate. We all smile and cry; we all live and die. We are all warmed and nurtured by the same sun. The sun doesn't discriminate. The sun is part of me,

Please Visit www.LifeTeamStrategy.com

part of you, so why should I discriminate? With pen in hand I contemplated the nondiscriminatory nature of the sun, to see what it could teach me.

> *As the eyelid on the horizon slowly opens for the dawn, its iris illuminates a new day. The darkness slowly withdraws, and life continues on. The rays of the sun envelop all things, rejecting none. They shine upon the pleasure as well as the suffering of this life. I am grateful to the sun for the life it helps create. It does so without judgment. It only patiently provides the support required for all things to grow, adapt and refine themselves. It doesn't hold a standard for who or what is worthy of its warmth. It simply provides an environment in which things can simply be as they are. The sun is not eclipsed by fear; it allows itself and others to shine. The eye of sunshine is crystal clear; perhaps my eyes can be so as well. As the sun sustains my life, I might as well absorb its character as well as its warmth.*

THE BIRD OF CHANGE

As I got stronger I was able to take longer walks before becoming fatigued. On several occasions I made my way to the city park. The leaves on the trees were beginning to turn, and I was so amazed by the vibrant colors that in the past I may have only regarded in passing. I saw colors I never knew existed because in the past I had no use for them. Sounds I once avoided I now appreciated as I really listened instead of letting them linger in the background.

I learned a lot in that park over the next month. When I was up to it, I would spend hours there. I would look, listen and feel the life around me. I would sit and listen to the animals and feel the wind blow as my breath moved in and out of my body. I closed my eyes and listened to the birds as they sang to each other and, seemingly, to me as well. It was amazing how this little thing called change could be responsible for so much beauty. I opened my eyes and saw one of the birds fly by. I realized that it was the change in the position of its wings as they met with the air that was responsible for this beauty. The change that I had so often fought against was now becoming my greatest teacher. I was later able to write down my observations.

> *All things begin and end with change; thusly, no things begin and end. When is there any pause or hesitation during which a thing may begin or end? Change when embraced brings peace, when we let go of that which doesn't belong to us. Change, when fought for or against, brings suffering and confusion when we fight against the inevitable.*

Please Visit www.LifeTeamStrategy.com

As I watched the bird fly by and thought of my own struggles adapting to change, I realized that the bird was free to fly as long as it worked with the wind instead of against it. Imagine what I could accomplish by riding the winds of change instead of trying to quiet them. I was feeling even more connected to everything around me. With so much around me nurturing my life, I knew I would never be alone again.

On another occasion I lied on the grass in the middle of the park and looked up at the trees. There were so many so close together that the colors changed quickly from red to yellow to green to orange as I moved my eyes across the row. It was like nature was given a giant canvas and went to work. I reflected on how I'd colored the canvas of my own life with values and expectations that severely skewed how things actually were. It was even more clear that I added something to everything in my life and not always something positive. Within myself I had an entire painter's palette of bright and dingy colors that I had splashed on the canvas of my life. But I would no longer foolishly and impulsively splash my life with the dark, gloomy paints of depression and fear. I had a whole palette to choose from. Wouldn't life be more interesting if each new day were a blank canvas until something was added to it? I only needed to make sure I painted more deliberately. Now it was time to begin the masterpiece that was to become my life.

Life was becoming brighter and brighter as I put faith in life to be my teacher instead of trying to have it all figured out all the time. In school I was always praised by the teacher for being right. In classroom discussions it was always important to ask the right questions and have the right answers. This often caused a fear of being wrong. People were censured and laughed at in class for being wrong. I was now beginning to see the strength and value in wrongness, or more precisely, in not trying to be always right.

F.E.A.R.

Through my experience with illness and looking back on what I had been taught about being right, I discovered that too much of my life had been lived in F.E.A.R.: Favoring Evidence Against Results. We experience F.E.A.R. when we **Shout** at ourselves by focusing on all the evidence that suggests our efforts will result in failure instead of success. A fear of taking action because you're afraid of failure is as foolish as not walking for fear you might fall. F.E.A.R. occurs when the **Shouter** in you drowns out the **Starter** in you.

Please Visit www.LifeTeamStrategy.com

We often learn that being wrong is shameful and not part of the learning process but a reflection of being unprepared or unable. Generating and exploring answers need to be recognized as processes of refining our knowledge. This makes more sense than frustrating ourselves into stopping before we begin out of fear.

I now actively seek out opportunities to get all misperceptions out of my head by asking questions. My focus isn't on whether I will appear ignorant; my focus is on learning something, and if I have a question, I will find the answer. I may occasionally stumble and even be laughed at by the ignorant and insecure in the pursuit of knowledge. But I always remember that there is no goal worth reaching that doesn't leave you postmarked from the trip.

True fear should be reserved for only two things: fight or flight. Fear is a survival instinct that serves us well. Disappointment is not life threatening, so why fear it? When we fear those things that threaten our ego, we value security over success. If you want to reach your goals, you have to fall and scrape your knees up a few times. This is the art of learning to walk. A bird may be born to fly, but that doesn't mean it has to get it right the first time.

After the loss of my friendships as well as my various illusions about life, I furiously punished myself because my perceptions had been wrong. The more I became acquainted with the ever-changing state of things, I came to realize that there was no right—there was only right now. Each moment of life clearly had its own issues to be resolved, and that would determine what was right now.

I spent too much time in my life, as have many **Shouters** I know, burying myself in self-doubt and insecurity and never going out of my way to breathe in as much life as possible. Unfortunately, it took almost losing my life to discover that if I want anything in life, I have to act and act now. The house is burning, and I have to get out. If I don't, I will suffer the consequences of my stubbornness and inaction.

As I became more in touch with how I had been responsible for the way I dealt with my illness, I accepted the tumors I was creating and what a **Shouter** I'd been. I began reflecting more on how I had traveled through life up to this point. Having ignored what was right now for so long, I wondered how many times I had done more harm than good when my own perception was my only consideration.

Please Visit www.LifeTeamStrategy.com

MARKING MY PATH

One day after a heavy rain, which seemed to clear up as quickly as it arose, I took another walk to the park. The ground was very soft, and I noticed how my feet were sinking into the ground, leaving an obvious trace of where I had been. I thought again about the mark I had left as I walked through life because of how I chose to carry myself. With this in mind, I contemplated the path I wanted to walk instead. There has been enough suffering in my life, and I was through causing it in my life and the lives of others. My Hara was now pointing in a new direction—one in which there is no turning back.

I will walk the path in its center, and its edges will not blunt. I need to stay centered and balanced. When I lose focus, I stumble and cut my feet on the edges. If doubts or the hurtful influence of the world around me become distracting, then I will veer off course. I must keep my eyes pointed in the direction I intend to go, not to the left nor to the right, and never looking back.

If I walk my path with my head bowed in shame, then the subsequent weight on my toes digs the walk of shame into the ground beneath me. Wherever I walk, shame walks with me. If I hold my nose upward with pride, the weight on my heels drives pride into my path as well as the paths of those I cross. As I lean toward one extreme it creates imbalance. Such extremes serve to corrupt and damage my ability to be flexible and adjust where needed.

I lose my balance forward in shame. I lose my balance backward with pride. Either way it is easier to knock me down because I am off balance. A walk of haste and impatience scares my path with the constant pushing off of my feet. A walk of sadness scares my path as my feet drag along. A walk of anger dents my path as my feet stomp along. A walk of procrastination gives a sag to my path as the weight of my feet remains too long in one place.

Walking my path in any extreme way will distort it. Thus by remaining centered no damage will be left. Without haste I make no step before the previous step is complete. Without haste there is no loss of balance and there is no hesitation in my step. My step may then be placed with even weight. Weight placed with care and not haste will not scratch the uncorrupted path but only provide a soft nurturing touch. I will take my time and not begin a new task before the previous one is finished. What kind of a future will I have if I don't do the best I can in the present?

Less and less I put a sense of importance on my selfish desires. For it was more obvious than ever that what I wanted did not hold the same importance as what was needed. For example, I may have gotten angry when it rained because my plans had been spoiled. But some farmers may have needed those rains so their crops could grow and their families could have money to put food on their tables. The animals may have needed it to avoid dehydration. The trees may have needed it to grow and produce oxygen so I could breathe and live. So, which is really more important, my trivial plans or the rain? Now when it rains, I can't help but smile.

So many things surround us, each with their own set of needs and wants. I will never be so arrogant as to assume I know what things are most important in life, because although I am a part of it, I didn't design it. What I can do is watch the things that are responsible for creating this life, and by watching what they do, I can learn what is most needed and which methods are most effective.

The very world we live in sustains us as we strive for success; we cannot be gluttonous as we proceed. In being so we deplete the very forces that we rely on to sustain us in our journey, and before long, they will not be able to hold us up any longer. Take care of and give each situation what it needs, then move on to what you need. Support all those around you, and the more you support them the more they will support you. Although my friends left me in my time of need, I now go out of my way to support as many people as I can. It can be something as small as a smile or a kind word or something as grand as the shirt off my back. I support them with what I have to give. I have no doubt that the support will be there when I need it.

Without variety, life could not happen. If there was only one custom or method, one direction or design, one color, one scent, only one single option, then what could change change into? Without variety, it could do nothing. Imagine a machine in a factory with rotating cogs joined by interlocking teeth. If every cog suddenly rotated clockwise, they would not move. They would all lock up as they competed against each other for movement. Without alternating rotation, no movement, no function can take place.

If every organ in the human body were only useful for the exact same function, then we would not survive. Each organ has its own specific shape and its own specific function. Through this wonderful variety of interaction, this interdependent function, a living being is able to sustain itself.

The more I learn, the more I have yet to learn. Now I can see a life more intricate and vast than before. It's amazing what lies before me now that I realize there is more to life than what goes on between my ears. The more I watch and learn from nature, the less I worry. No matter what problems I have in life, everything still seems to be taken care of. The sun rises and sets, and the world keeps on turning. I realize that I'm but one piece of the great puzzle of life. I am not responsible for the whole puzzle but only for what my piece provides toward maintaining the stability of the whole. I don't have to worry about controlling so much of my life because I never had control in the first place; I only had a desire for it. I couldn't control my birth; I can't prevent my death. I can't change the weather or the actions of others, because these things are out of my hands.

Understanding this has far-reaching consequences. With no room to make excuses, thoughtfulness is essential. In all of my relationships, I can choose and am responsible for everything I bring to each relationship. I can decide to increase the suffering in life with what I bring or I can choose to reduce it. It's my choice what I give to this life and only my responsibility to live it. No one can make me do anything.

I was responsible for how I felt when my friends left me, and I was responsible for how I reacted. At the time I blamed them for how I felt. I was caught up in the "they made me do it" rant of a **Shouter**. The reason my emotional pain didn't go away during that time was because I was too busy placing blame when the responsibility was mine. I was essentially waiting around for someone else to come along and solve my problems. It was like spraying water on the smoke to put out the fire. Now I have found tremendous freedom in taking responsibility for myself. In taking charge, peer pressure isn't a factor because I realize that any choice I make is my own. No longer is my mind filled with the blame of holding others responsible for my life or the guilt of having let others talk me into something I now regret.

BEING MYSELF

By being true to myself, I am left to act with deeper conviction and confidence. If I choose to treat people well, then nothing they do should change that. If I am kind to someone and they treat me like crap, then I made my choice of what I would bring to that situation and they made theirs. In the past I may have gotten angry with them because I would have felt I deserved to be treated nicely, too. But I cannot make someone else's decisions for them. If I choose to be pleasant, there is no reason why I should be talked out of it. But it is important to respect the other person's responsibility to make their choice.

As I continue to watch and learn, I gain a greater awareness of just how much is contributed to life because things are just being themselves. I observe how the sun warms the earth because it is just being responsible for being the sun, which is the same for the tree, the ocean and even me. How much could I give to this life by just being myself? It's inspiring to see what power lies in doing something so simple.

In thinking about what being myself meant, I was able to resolve an issue that still lingered in the back of my mind: the feeling of being incomplete because I now only had one testicle. I felt a little freakish with my bald head and perceived inadequacies. But as I discovered the wonder of variety and the strength that comes with that variety, my insecurities about this issue disappeared. I discovered that who I am as a person and as a man comes from being the man I am. I had to contribute my unique brand of masculinity and humanity to this world in whatever form it came in. It wasn't my responsibility to be the definition of masculinity I had come to know. One testicle or five, I was still myself and that defined my value—not the packaging I was presently dressed in but the value of its contents.

How wonderful it is to take responsibility for who and what I am. I mentioned before that I was now taking responsibility for everything I brought to the relationships in my life. The more I thought about this, the more I thought about the kind of friend I could be to others by simply giving what I could. My friends had left me when I was in need. That was their choice. At this point I made a promise to myself that if I ever had the opportunity to reduce the suffering in someone else's life, I would not pass it up. That is my choice.

I could have used a friend like that. So now I am determined to be a friend like that. Although it's always preferable to get what you give, I have stated many times that that is not what occurred in my situation. I now give because I choose to, not because I expect a return.

My life is becoming more simplified. As I gradually relinquish my obsession with the past, I realize more what is my business and let go of what isn't. By doing this, life becomes more manageable. Like the tree, I live more in the present. I take life one moment at a time, mostly because that's the only way it comes. It's amazing how when you handle life the way it's dished out, it is much more manageable and less stressful.

When I was going through my experience with cancer, I enveloped myself in the entirety of all of my wants and fears. I don't remember once taking things one moment at a time. Instead I would long for the past and wish for or fear the future instead of tending to the present. The best way I can describe how I went from worrying about everything at once and learning to take life one moment at a time, in addition to the bending of the tree, lies in the process of assembling a puzzle.

Please Visit www.LifeTeamStrategy.com

Life is a giant puzzle, but an immensely manageable one. And we all contribute a valuable piece. As each new day passes and I come more to terms with what happened and what it all means to me, I feel the pain of my ordeal fade further and further away. I was raised to believe that pain and its expression was a sign of weakness and was essentially the enemy of strength and good character. It was a long time before I saw my pain clearly enough to realize that it could be used as fertile soil from which new life could emerge.

A Crack in the Soil

I watched my grandfather harvest his small garden the summer after my chemo ended. As he would tear the roots from the ground, a small hole would remain where life had once flourished. But the next year he would be planting new seeds in those same holes so life could begin again. This was another lesson I was beginning to learn. Each hole that was dug in my spirit with every loss I endured could now support a new bud of life sprouting where a seed of hope was planted. It may be a sign of strength to endure pain, but it's also equally, if not more valuable, to learn and grow from it.

I began seeing the earth and soil in a new way. During the summer I would notice it all dried out from drought, pale and riddled with cracks. It appeared to be breaking from the dryness of the heat. It seemed to be opening itself up, becoming more vulnerable, weakening. Or was this a sign of its strength?

In opening wide to the coming rains, the cracks allow the soil to be thoroughly filled with water. It would appear that opening myself up would allow me to be nourished and filled with what I needed as well. If I close myself in fear that I might be hurt, then I am likely to shut out that which might also help me grow.

This is more an example of the soils' strength than vulnerability. It allows itself the help it needs for continued vitality. The soil regains its consistency, its strength and its fertility through its openness.

The soil also allows seeds to enter it. Then before you know it, within this vulnerability a seed is planted and new life begins to grow. I know now what appears as vulnerability is an opening in which life can begin. I'm filled with soil, potential and an endless number of openings from which new growth can sprout. Like my grandfather's garden, I need only to allow in the seeds that will help me grow.

One of the hardest lessons to swallow throughout all of this was not only learning to trust enough to allow hope to take root, but also to realize that there is a time when I must let go of the past and the things I loved there. Although the losses I suffered were great, had I not endured them, I wouldn't have the quality of life I do now. I would not be the man I am today.

As I watch the things in my everyday life pass, I realize there is nothing in life that I can ever possess. I can only possess the experience of these things. I now understand that everything passes, nothing stays the same. Everything is temporary. So what is it that I thought I had? I realized that the things I suffered the greatest sense of loss from were the things I thought were mine, including my friends, my girlfriend and my life. How silly was I to think I owned something that I couldn't keep? Everything I had experienced was simply that: a passing experience. So obviously there was nothing there to be possessed. But there was and is plenty to be experienced.

Whether it is a car, a sunset, a relationship with a loved one or the very life I live, the secret to enjoying something is not in having it but in experiencing it. When something does finally pass, I will hopefully not suffer as much as I would have, had I expected it to stay.

As I said before, the more I learn, the more I have left to learn. I will never be an expert in this life because my life is a work in progress, an evolving work that requires patience, diligence and an eye for detail. I will carry on as a perpetual student. For with every passing breath, I learn more about myself and what life has in store for me. Experience has always been the greatest teacher. My life is the greatest reward. As I continue on my journey, I will do so as a dedicated and eager student of life. I leave this section of the book with the oath I follow as I learn: I will always remember to learn and grow and never be corrupted by what I think I know.

I want to close Part One of this book with a short tribute to my grandfather. During my cancer treatment there was one other person besides my mother who was especially good to me: my mother's father, my grandfather. Every time I would visit his home he would grab my hand with a firm handshake and a joyful smile and say, "How are you doing boy? I'm really proud of you. Stick with it, you're doing great" or some variation of that. He would say this to me in a room full of relatives that would make a bee line to my mother and ask, "How's he doing?" when I was 20 feet away and perfectly capable of answering for myself.

One of the many days I sat and watched him garden I took the time to thank him. I thanked him for his support and told him how much it meant to me and helped me keep my chin up. I also made him a promise, that "If I ever have a son I will name him after you." I made this promise not knowing whether I'd be able to have children, a possibility my doctors warned me about.

Please Visit www.LifeTeamStrategy.com

Several years later my grandfather died and I did not forget my promise to him. For several years after he passed I met and married my dear wife, Katie. To both of our shear delight, three months after we were married Katie came to me with the surprising news that she was pregnant, even more surprising because she had been on the Pill. What was that about not having kids again, doc? When we found out during an ultrasound that we would be having a boy, I told Katie of the promise I made to my grandfather and she supported it 100%. When my son was born he was given the first name Zachary, and my grandfather's Romanian birth name Vasile. I kept my promise to a man whose simple encouragement had meant so much. I love you, Grandpa.

PART II
A Cure for What Ails You

*Walking the path of life successfully
begins with a simple technique.
Put one foot in front of the other,
and do it with confidence.*

3

The Responsibility Cure

What you read in Part One was only meant to tweak your brain and prepare you for the work to be done. So do you feel primed? It is now time to get down to business and start putting the cure to work. The rest of this book instructs you in a series of techniques and observations that will lead you through the process of developing and embodying a mindset that will not only allow you to unscrew yourself but ideally prevent you from becoming totally screwed ever again.

Before you read further, you may want to ask yourself the same question that I did. In the story of your life, are you a victim or a victor? Victim's are **Shouters,** and Victors are **Starters**. Remember that you can **Start** in one area of your life and **Shout** in another.

Reinhold Neibuhr wrote, "Grant me the serenity to accept the things I cannot change, courage to change the things I can, and wisdom to know the difference." Although I haven't been on this planet very long, I have acquired a lot of mileage. I believe I can address the desire to learn to accept the things you cannot change, identify the things you can change (the courage to change them is up to you) and begin to understand the difference.

I've learned that all I can really count on is the present. I contemplated for some time how my life was seemingly out of control and how I couldn't determine what, if any, kind of control I had over my circumstances. When I began looking to myself for what I could do to create the change I wanted, it finally hit me: I had complete control over two things, control that couldn't be taken from me by any means, no matter what my circumstances. By taking responsibility for these two things, I realized I would be able to regain control over my life. This realization is explained by what I call "The Two Responsibilities."

Referring back to Mr. Neibuhr's statement, these two responsibilities are the things that I can change and can control. All other things then are the things I cannot change. As you read and embrace the concepts I will share with you, you will begin to acquire the wisdom to know the difference between the two. Mastering your "Two Responsibilities" is the first step in your journey to becoming unscrewed. I'll also share several ideas with you that will help you accept the things you cannot change more easily. We will begin with a little exercise.

TAKING RESPONSIBILITY AND TAKING CONTROL

On the lines provided below, list a maximum of ten of your greatest responsibilities in life right now.

1._____
2._____
3._____
4._____
5._____
6._____
7._____
8._____
9._____
10._____

Now that your list is completed, ask yourself the following questions:

How many did you list?

How many of the responsibilities involve meeting the expectations of other people?

How many of the responsibilities require the cooperation of factors that are out of your control?

How many of the responsibilities could be difficult to carry out because of interference from factors out of your control?

Review your list carefully, and choose the one responsibility that causes you the greatest amount of stress (mental, physical and/or emotional discomfort) and difficulty. Which responsibility seems to be the greatest source of exhaustion or is in some other way harmful to you? Keep this responsibility in mind as we proceed. Since this responsibility causes you the most difficulty, applying the following concepts to it should make it easier for you when it comes time to apply them to less complicated tasks.

Referring back to the previous list of questions, I would suggest to you that all of your responsibilities contain some elements that are out of your control. In fact, accomplishing even the smallest tasks throughout our day is dependent upon factors we take for granted and can do nothing about. For example, my ability to complete the morning routine that prepares me for the day depends upon the presence of running water, the electricity being on, having clothes to wear, food to eat, etc. The experience of stress begins with our attitude toward the uncontrollable aspects of our lives. How much of your day do you think is spent fretting over unfulfilled responsibilities that were derailed by things you couldn't control even if you wanted to?

A few people I've met were very domineering **Shovers** due to their desire to control anything and everything, including the people around them. One way these **Shovers** attempt to control others is by taking on the problems of others as their own. This clearly is an infringement on the rights of others in favor of one's own desires. The main problems with this idea is that we cannot solve other people's problems for them no matter how hard we work at it nor do we allow ourselves the time to deal with our own. This unachievable role of global caretaker eats away at the one who takes it on. But there is a way of unscrewing oneself from this **Shover** role.

One way this **Shover** role eats away at us is when something doesn't get done or doesn't go right. We then get mad at it for not going our way or become angry at ourselves for not having more control where we think we should. We are often personally offended when the world doesn't operate at our discretion. For example, when you're in a hurry in your car because you have a responsibility to get somewhere at a certain time and a red light catches you, what are you mad at? You're mad at the light because it interfered with your progress, right? Why? It has nothing to do with you; it's not personal, and it's something you can't do anything about. Nonetheless, our minds begin spinning with a stress-inducing internal dialogue about what the red light means in the course of our progress. Comments such as "Almost made it" leaves one feeling like the light beat you in some kind of competition. This is just one small example of how the manner in which we relate to the uncontrollables in our lives can determine the quality of our day and the amount of stress in it.

This kind of thinking is also what resulted in my anger toward my friends for not treating me the way I expected them to when I had cancer. It is the **Shover** mind that states everything has to go my way for my benefit at all times or something is terribly wrong with the world. As absurd as this thinking is, we still do it. Some of us do it some of the time, others most of the time. Take an inventory of all of your reactions today, and see how many of them stem from an inflated need to control.

YOUR LOCUS OF CONTROL

There are many assumptions or expectations we use to influence our perceptions of the countless uncontrollables in our everyday lives. Often assumptions can vary from person to person since our self-talk varies. These assumptions arise in part from the perception that our experiences originate outside of ourselves and thus happen to us. This is referred to as an "external locus of control," which means you perceive that forces outside of yourself influence and control your life. Let's see if we can begin to think about this a new way.

First of all, nothing is ever outside us. As soon as we react to something, it is inside us. It has entered our experience, and we undergo a change as a result of our experience of it. Whether it is the red light we took in, a warm breeze, a kind word or a not so kind word, nothing that catches our attention happens outside of us. Our experiences and the lessons of our lives result from what we do with what we take in to ourselves.

A person who takes full responsibility for their own experiences has an "internal locus of control," which is the realization that they may not control the events of their lives but they do control their responses to them. The easiest way to demonstrate how the internal locus of control works is by using an equation I learned from one of my mentors, Jack Canfield (Co creator of the *Chicken Soup for the Soul* series). The equation states that $E + R = O$. There are *E*vents in your life and your *R*esponses to them, which equal the *O*utcomes you experience as a result of your responses to the events (Canfield, 2000). You can use this equation to gauge your responses in any situation.

Please Visit www.LifeTeamStrategy.com

While experiencing cancer treatment I clearly had an external locus of control. I believed that my anger and depression was everybody else's fault because of how they were treating me. There's some real **Shouter** thinking for you. But when I began to understand that my feelings were the outcomes of my responses to how they were treating me, I took responsibility for them and acquired an internal locus of control. When you're able to do this you'll discover as I did that your circumstances are never bigger than you are. You may not be able to control what happens around you, but you can control what happens inside you.

Not only can you choose the response you will have, but in doing so, you can actually change the outcome. Think of the $E + R = O$ equation in terms of $2 + 2 = 4$. If you always respond the same way to the same event, you will experience the same outcome. So, $2 + 2$ will always equal 4. But if you change your response you change the outcome. So now your equation might read $2 + 3 = 5$ (Canfield, 2000). Simple, huh? In the bigger scheme of things, you can literally change your life simply by changing your mind. You've just learned a basic way to change **Shover** or **Shouter** thinking into **Starter** thinking.

When we focus on the things we want to control but are unable to, then the things we actually do have control over tend to be the things we expend the least amount of energy on influencing. But that can all change right now. What if you could construct your life so that every responsibility you had contained only those elements that were totally in your control? You'd be able to go from Totally Screwed to Total Control. You'd no longer stress about the other things, and life would be simpler and less stressful. Believe it or not, there is a way to do this.

Refer back to your list of responsibilities at the beginning of this exercise. In spite of the amount of responsibilities you may have listed, I am going to suggest to you that there are only two responsibilities you are capable of following through on consistently and guaranteeing the results. And I'll bet neither of them appears on your list. I firmly believe that these responsibilities are the only two you will ever need to accomplish day to day, and they will allow you to accomplish all that you need to on any given day. And because these two responsibilities exist in every activity of your life, you can have total control when it comes to fulfilling them.

These two responsibilities emerge from and are nurtured by your Hara, the foundation of who you are. If you can master these two responsibilities, your ability to focus your energies and increase your effectiveness in any situation will open like a floodgate. Here we go.

Please Visit www.LifeTeamStrategy.com

YOUR RESPONSIBILITIES

The two things in life you are responsible for are **who you are** and **what you do**. Now, before you read on, you need to make a personal commitment to take 100% responsibility for these areas of your life. No doubts, no reservations, no excuses. Unless you take these responsibilities in your hands, the rest will be next to impossible to accomplish. Did you commit? Are you ready? Okay, keep going.

Who you are refers to your Self:

a. All of your beliefs, values and attitudes

b. Perceptions, assumptions, expectations about yourself and others

c. All other impressions that guide and inspire your navigation through this life

What you do refers to your Actions:

- The things you say and do as a result of **who you are**, your "Responses"
- Your behavior, actions, the outcomes you help create

Remember, you can pick and choose your beliefs, indulge in whatever attitude you like. These two responsibilities are the foundation of your internal locus of control because you only truly feel in control of your life when you take control where you have it.

What you do is best expressed in what you say to yourself, also referred to as the "internal coach" or "internal critic." The first has the voice of a **Starter**; the other the voice of a **Shouter**. These voices express your own opinion of your worth. The coach empowers, the critic condemns.

Your two responsibilities are at the heart of your being; they are fueled by your Hara. So if what you do is more critical than complimentary, then that influences the direction your life takes. Your critic saps the energy that could otherwise be used for progress and uses it to fuel doubt and discouragement. Think of it as buying an airplane that never has enough power to take off and fly.

Remember what I said earlier about thinking from your Hara? I hope it is evident that **who you are** as I've described it stems from thought and not instinct—the brain instead of the gut. I'd be surprised if I met a person who claimed that relying on his or her brain exclusively didn't get them in trouble on a regular basis.

Please Visit www.LifeTeamStrategy.com

Again, I point out that learning to be guided by your Hara will create an increased tendency toward certainty in your decision-making. The more certain you are, the more likely you are to follow through, as any **Starter** would. Remember that your Hara is your source of balance. Your Hara prefers balance—that is why you get the queasy feeling in a situation that your brain says is okay but your gut is warning you about. Your brain lacks the sensitivity your Hara has.

Important note: The queasiness I'm talking about here is not the butterflies you feel when your brain is engaged in negative self-talk that is causing you to worry. If that's where the queasiness is coming from, then there is usually no other danger than that which you create for yourself. One example of the queasiness I am talking about is that early warning sign of danger. I've been in a few traffic accidents where my Hara tightened up a few seconds before I was hit, and I had no idea the hit was coming. You can also experience tightness in your Hara that pushes you to act in a positive way—a gut feeling that tells you you're doing the right thing. I've heard people who run into burning houses to help people escape describe a tingling in their bellies that pulled them toward the house. This is the Hara telling you your actions will have a safe outcome.

To assist you in letting go of the hold your ***who you are*** programming has on you, it is important to realize that beliefs are inherently disposable. The programming that makes you you is a work in progress, undergoing constant revision and transformation at your discretion. John C. Lilly said that "Every belief is a limit to be examined and transcended" (Canfield, 2000). Moshe Feldenkrais also recognized that "The only thing permanent about our behavior patterns is our belief that they are so" (Canfield, 2000).

Remember, limiting beliefs are detrimental to us, especially the belief that we have limits. If this were true, we'd be capable of so little growth that we'd proceed through life virtually unchanged.

The truth of the matter is that none of us is the same as we were the day we left our mother's womb. We have all undergone a substantial change process and continue to do so. The butterfly may undergo the transformation process only once, but we can do it daily or moment to moment to whatever degree we choose. As we encounter new experiences, information and education, we're offered opportunities to refine who we are. **Starters** seek out and embrace these opportunities; **Shouters** fear them.

Consider your life a story that is always being written and rewritten, with new characters entering and leaving the story daily. In a way, your beliefs are characters in your story. They guide the action by setting the rules for how you as the main character will proceed. They tell you what your options are. Your beliefs determine what is meaningful and what is trivial. A simple example of this would be if you believe that people who call you names are bad or mean. You feel this way because you believe that there are such things as insults and that they are rightfully perceived as negative. This belief usually results in the response called being offended.

An alternative belief would be that statements made by others are opinions, based solely on the rules of their story. Just because somebody throws something at you doesn't mean you have to catch it. You can decide how or even whether to invest yourself in another person's words or actions.

As I said, like any character in a story your beliefs will come and go. Growth is a result of adjustments to changes in your circumstances. Growth in plants results from its response to the presence of water and sunlight. We grow from the presence of positive forces in our lives or other experiences that force us to make adjustments.

Beliefs are characters that come in and out; they can also be seen as tools used by you, the master carpenter for shaping your reality into the work of art you envision for yourself. As such, they should only be tools you can use to accomplish your goals. More importantly, you need to be in control of your tools—not the other way around. If your beliefs/tools control you, especially when that control results in a negative outcome, then it's time to throw them out and replace them with tools you can use. Tools can become old, blunted, worn out or in all other ways less effective. So if you can't use it, lose it. If you weigh yourself down with a lot of stuff that is of no use, then what do you become? I don't recall a time in my life when clutter has ever been to my advantage.

You choose your tools, you write the story, you decide what to splash on the canvas that makes you who you are, and your actions are a direct result of that. So, clearly who you are and what you do are your responsibilities alone. This is the time when people usually bring up all the excuses they can as to why their parents or any other person are actually responsible for the way they are. My all-purpose response to that assertion is that your parents are responsible for their contributions to your life, but you are responsible for your response to them. As children we usually lack the self-awareness to process what is happening around us or our reactions to it. But once we are aware, we hold all of the cards and all of the responsibility for changing the outcome or keeping it the same. At this point, excuses lack any credibility. Whatever judgment you may make regarding your experiences, how you process them and what you give back to the world in response lies squarely on your shoulders.

In spite of what we are used to thinking, our beliefs and attitudes are no more who we are than a carpenter is his tools or a dancer is her feet. It is how we use these things that makes us who we are. Who we are, as I said earlier, is a work in progress. Our lives can only become whatever our current beliefs or attitudes allow us to conceive for ourselves. A carpenter's tools may become lost or broken, but an artist and the art never die. Beethoven wasn't defeated by his deafness because the music was in his heart not his ears.

Don't hold so tightly to your thoughts, theories and beliefs, because they change and grow as readily as you do. They are instruments that guide us, like a steering wheel guides a car. We are not our beliefs, and the car is not the road. What matters is our willingness to adjust as the road changes. When we mistake our beliefs for who we are, we close the door to growth. We mistake our cocoon for the world, not considering the option of leaving it. It's time to break out.

By choosing to embrace this new thinking, you'll have to give up a few things like blaming other people or other things for your thoughts and reactions. No longer can you say "that makes me mad"; what actually occurred was you got mad, you chose that response. The "they made me do it" defense is a thing of the past. The processing and emotional response to an event result from the value or meaning you place on the experience and are, therefore, completely your doing. In other words, you're choosing to engage in the activity of anger, sadness, etc, in response to an event. You weren't given anger by something; you're giving anger to it.

GIVING YOUR MIND AWAY

Assigning blame or responsibility to others for the things you have control over is something **Shouters** do that I call "giving your mind away." This is something we do quite readily and far too often. Giving your mind away means giving control of yourself over to others. This applies mostly to allowing others to manipulate our thoughts and emotions. I spent 18 years of my life doing this, and I've met others who do it until the day they die. We give power to others over our emotions, allowing our hearts to become their personal gymnasiums to play whatever games they like. The more of your mind you give away, the less you keep for yourself to use for reaching your goals because you give someone else too many of the strings to pull.

Furthermore, it's just plain careless to primarily look to others to tell us what to think and believe. If that person's word is all you have to go on, then you walk

Please Visit www.LifeTeamStrategy.com

around being guided by a belief that has no foundation. As you know, something built without a foundation doesn't stand very long. "So and so said it was true," is not a good reason to believe something. Not to mention, if this person is the only source of that belief, then you must run to them for their counsel, and they determine when the belief should be adjusted. Of course, it is important to seek the guidance of others in matters you're unfamiliar with. But when it comes to your two responsibilities, don't give power to someone else, especially over the only two areas of your life where you have complete control. The more control over yourself you give away, the less you have of yourself to give to others.

I understand how easy it is to have your mind taken from you by the countless distractions we face every day. Later in the book when you practice the exercise called Minding the Breath, you'll learn to be able to tell when your mind is leaving you. When your mind wanders and becomes distracted, your task is to get it back. Whenever you feel overwhelmed and out of control, your goal is to stay in control of yourself; self-control is the only real control you can ever have. As you read, I will introduce to you ways in which increasing self-control and thus control of your life direction is done.

The Search for Security

One of the biggest thieves of our mind is our endless search for security in life. We seek comfort, safety and certainty in all walks of life. The problem here is that we strive for something that doesn't exist. In other words, "If it can be taken from you, it isn't yours." I don't speak merely of material things but of living things as well. My life clearly isn't mine—I didn't choose my birth, and I don't know when it will end, but I do bear the responsibility for what I do and create with it. My wife is not mine, although we entered into an agreement that we will be by each other's side forever. I will lose her someday, whether it be "till death do us part" or some other reason, so I must never be complacent when it comes to enjoying and valuing her presence in my life.

I also believe this search for security is the root of human suffering. This search drives us to try and hold on to what we want or to avoid what we don't want. Besides our two responsibilities, everything can be taken from us. No matter how much we care for or come to depend upon something or someone, it will leave at some point. The main reason we experience loss in life is because we come to count on something's continued presence for our well-being, which is an unreasonable expectation. Things move in and out of our lives, and we need to understand their impermanence if we are to benefit from their presence while we have them.

Trying to avoid the things we don't want is foolish as well. Once I was diagnosed with cancer, I could not want it with all my heart. The not wanting what was unavoidable could only serve to increase my suffering, and it certainly did. What was the lesson we learned earlier? If you can't change the event, then change your response to it. One of my best friends is always stating how she doesn't deal well with change. When I hear this from her or anyone else, I am amazed by what a blatant misattribution it is of the real issue. Change isn't the problem; it is effortless. It's happening this moment on a massive scale. What they have a problem with is challenges to their need for security. When their security is threatened, they blame change instead of realizing that it is their own expectations that are problematic.

If we so desire we can continue to run and hide and otherwise avoid the things we don't like. But as I said, it is the avoidance of these negative things that causes us pain and suffering. When we find we can't avoid them, we feel like something is wrong with us. "Why do bad things keep happening? I'm a good person. They shouldn't happen to me." Well, why not? The person you are has more to do with how you meet the challenges in your life, not whether you have them or not.

What often happens is, the more we realize we are unable to find the security we seek, the more we slowly begin to close ourselves off, and our unwillingness to take risks causes us to shrink into a little subjective fish bowl. We fear trying anything that might result in failure or loss, and as a result, we stick only to those things that up to that point have been consistent. We do our job the same old way; we keep on having the same old day. The difference between the employer and the employee is that the employer focuses on increasing success, which is fueled by embracing change and taking risks, while the employee focuses on increasing security by reducing risks and minimizing change.

So when someone asks, "What's new?" most people respond, "Nothing." If that's your answer, then that's your fault. You have effectively worked yourself into a rut of complacency in order to maintain an illusion of security and certainty. You're pretty screwed if you ask me. Complacency is the enemy of growth. You spend all of your time doing and little or none of it being. It is time to start thinking bigger; you have to step out of the fishbowl. The person who said, "The sky's the limit" wasn't thinking big enough. In my way of thinking, the sky is only the beginning. Although I wouldn't recommend it, it took a physical tumor to smash my fishbowl and put me in a situation where either I learned

Please Visit www.LifeTeamStrategy.com

how to survive in an environment without the fishbowl or I suffocated and died. Obviously, I chose to learn how to breathe air again.

If you sit around and try to hang on to everything, you will acquire a lot—a lot of selfishness, distrust and insecurity. The trick is in giving yourself permission to let go of something you couldn't keep in the first place. This will allow you to run freely in the direction of what you want without fear of loss, because in letting go, you don't value the idea of security—you value success. Success is about taking risks and moving on, striving for new things. **Shouters** live in a present that is clouded by the past. **Starters** live in a present filled with possibilities regardless of the past. It's time to build success.

Examine Your Expectations

As I mentioned earlier, our minds are routinely taken from us, mostly as a result of our own butterfingers. One of the ways is by accepting the **Shouting** of others that isn't designed to help us. We are often subjected to the fears and prejudices someone has created in their own minds to help further their efforts at maintaining security in their own lives. They in turn inflict these thoughts upon us, and these thoughts become our templates for dealing with the world. Your mind is only yours when you participate. So ask yourself, are you the puppet or the puppeteer? When you talk to yourself, who's doing the talking? Examine the rules and criticisms in your head, and determine where they came from. When someone tells me they only believe something because that's how they were raised, I always say, "Well who taught you that? And how well did it work for that person?" Believe it or not, most people never stop to do that and spend a lifetime following bad advice.

One pervasively rotten example to follow is the instruction given by an organization that instructs its members what to be offended by, how to express the offense and what to do with it. This is instruction in Victim 101 and is an example of how to give your mind away. Anytime you take offense to a particular use of language or a differing viewpoint, take a brief moment, breathe and do some self-examination. You'll quickly realize that in most cases the issue is in your response. Ask yourself where the threat in that statement or event was. Should others around you take responsibility for saying only the things you like? Should you be responsible for keeping others' attitudes in line? I would say none of the above. Unless we decide to compile a guidebook to our own emotional baggage

Please Visit www.LifeTeamStrategy.com

to hand out to everyone so they'll know what will offend us and what will make us happy, we might want to do some personal maintenance.

For starters, you need to realize that at least part of the threat lies in noncompliance with your expectations, or shoulds. Where did you learn to respond in this way? I learned it by being raised around selfish people who always insisted on things going their way. They taught me to be selfish as well. Since I felt I never got things my way, I insisted upon it whenever I felt I had a chance to do so.

Fortunately, I learned at some point that shoulds are preferences not imperatives, and I became more able to stop shoulding all over the place and learned to focus on my true responsibilities. Remember that you're responsible for who you are and what you do. Whatever anyone else chooses to contribute to the world is his or her responsibility. Your responsibility is for your contribution. We must focus solely on that which we can control and not be so preoccupied with the contributions of others. Our expectations, when not examined for their validity, can cause a great deal of difficulty. Your expectations can make you intolerant if you believe you deserve a certain outcome. Thus you judge and react harshly to others who seem to be doing better than you are.

Embracing your two responsibilities will bring greater peace of mind. It is comforting to go into every situation knowing what you're responsibilities are. The rest can only take care of itself. When concentrating on the two things you can control, you can execute them with complete precision and excellence because they have your undivided attention.

Of course, simply shifting your attention from the myriad things we typically concern ourselves with to only two is not an easy task. There are several rules that people in general have acquired that prevent them from doing this. For example, many people believe that their ability to impress people is somehow tied into their self-worth. They may believe that they are entitled to anything they want and that anything less is unacceptable. Another example is that if anything bad happens in their life, then something must be wrong with them or they're being punished somehow. All of these beliefs put primary importance on your expectations being met by factors that are out of your control. In addition, several of these beliefs depend upon the approval of others as a measure of our own value. This is why these beliefs result in so much stress and disappointment. They set standards that are both impossible and not worth living up to.

When instead we decide to be responsible for who we are and what we do, we have the final say in what we are going to contribute to life on a daily basis and what we allow it to contribute to us. If a coworker is miserable and wants to take it out on everybody else, fine. That's what he wants to contribute. If you want to be happy and complimentary all day, that's what you want to contribute and that's your responsibility. Your attitude requires your own tenacity and commitment to follow through on it—not whether others share it or not.

While completing my undergraduate degree I worked in a hospital that would become very busy very quickly. This most often brought out the worst in people as they became overwhelmed and impatient. I would decide before even going to work that I would contribute positively to the day; behaving otherwise simply wasn't a consideration. I was now living from my Hara, and my two responsibilities were all I needed to reinforce my decision. One particular day that stands out in my memory was when a fellow coworker with the same attitude as mine asked me how my day was going. I responded, "My day is going great. I've tripped over a few miserable people along the way, but I'm great." The point being, I don't care how stressful your workplace is or how crabby your coworkers and boss are, especially if they are compelled to take it out on you, because they are **Shouting** from their external locus of control. All they are doing is demonstrating the day they're having and their inability to deal with it; you're not having that kind of a day, so why join them? Have your day.

Whether life provides you with all you desire or protects you from suffering is hardly a measurement of your success or value. Whether you are victorious or defeated, the true value lies in what you do with either result. For example, a few years ago I was watching a newscast where the reporter was interviewing a farmer who'd just had his farm destroyed by a tornado. When the reporter asked him if he ever asked himself, "Why me?" his instantaneous reply was, "I never ask, why me? I only ask, what can I learn from it?" Do you see my point? Victory shows you what you did right; defeat shows you what you need to do differently next time or the things you can do nothing about. A defeat never means the journey is over, it just means it's a do-over. Somebody who comes in second in a race can either say they lost first or won second. Which compels you to learn and grow?

Success is an ongoing process punctuated by goal attainment. I have a problem with the thinking some people engage in that ties their self-worth to the outcome of a single event, whether it be one exam, one game, whatever. The object is to repair the flat and keep on driving. You don't give up based on one imperfect result, especially one that can be improved upon. You need to focus on the fix not the problem. Concentrate your energy on a problem only long enough to identify it. Then quickly move on to solving it. If a house is on fire, what good is it to stand around and say to yourself, "You know what, that house is on fire. Yep, it's on fire. Wow, look at that sucker burn. Man, I sure feel bad about it." You're clearly focusing on the problem not the solution. The victim who gets

Please Visit www.LifeTeamStrategy.com

burned does nothing but stand around and feel bad about the problem; the hero focuses on the solution and takes action to resolve the problem. When you want success, blame and fault finding doesn't help, it only preoccupies you and keeps you from moving on. Focus on the fix already, and get back to striving for success.

Embracing and maximizing your control over your two responsibilities will help you fully function in any social situation, whether it is familiar or completely brand new. What are the two aspects of any situation that you have control over? Who you are and what you do. I hear a lot of people say, "But I want to make a good impression." Well, let me ask you, where is a good impression made? In the other person's mind, that's where. Are we mind readers? How are we to know what will make a good impression? If we understand our two responsibilities, then we are unlikely to be overtly disrespectful, offensive or make a bad impression. If we accept responsibility for what we do, how many would choose to cause unpleasantness in someone else's day? Especially when we can no longer make excuses for it, since it is our responsibility, our choice. In trying to impress when you don't know what impression to make, you tend to operate as though you know what will please this other person, and your behaviors become contrived. The likelihood that your efforts will backfire increases when you try to master those factors that are none of your business instead of focusing on the factors that are.

Whenever you set a personal goal that's success is dependent on another person's unpredictable reaction, you're not likely to get it. There's no way of gauging someone else's reaction to you. When you manufacture a lot of good qualities to offer someone, hoping it's what they want, it typically comes across as phony. Let me ask you this: How hard is it to spot a salesperson? You can tell when you're being sold something, right? Well, if someone else senses a sales pitch coming from you, it can seem dishonest and make him or her suspicious. This may make them turn off to you, which I'm sure is the opposite of what you want. But by sticking to your two responsibilities, you put no pressure on yourself to contribute more than you already have. You can offer who you are and what you do to every situation in life, which is all you've got. You will be genuine, confident, relaxed and completely yourself. So put it out there honestly and confidently, and let any impression to be made take care of itself.

In nature, when everything is simply itself and makes its own unique contribution, then life is allowed to be at its very best. When the sun rises it's just being itself, and as a result, the earth is warmed and life is sustained. The warmth from the sun causes water to evaporate and become a cloud. When the cloud has too much water, it rains and it rains because the cloud is just being a cloud, and therefore, plants are watered and encouraged to grow. This natural process is so simple and yet so profoundly valuable.

Being human is just like this. When you feel sad, you cry; when you're happy, you laugh. When emotion becomes excessive, you cry, laugh, whatever, to release it. As a cloud rains its excess away, so do you. What remains is simply you. So when inspired to spread kindness, do so. When compelled to share, give. When grateful, love. Just simply be who you are. So much joy is added to life from these simple acts. All things in life—the sun, the earth, trees, flowers, human beings—exist in their most beautiful state when they are doing nothing more than being themselves. See how powerful a force just being true to your inherent responsibilities can be.

Who we are takes a lot of self-examination to determine. But it is essential to do so, because who we are determines every aspect of our lives. There are plenty of ideas in our heads that serve no other purpose than to make our lives more complicated. They hurt when what we actually need is help. It is up to you to confront those aspects of your programming that are outdated, untrue, harmful and just plain useless. The programming we choose to indulge in means the difference between success in life and failure. We succeed when we are able to accomplish the goals we set for ourselves and, more importantly, when we can contribute positively to the lives of those around us in the process. If you deliberately leave suffering in your wake, you have nothing to teach about success, I don't care what your balance sheet says. If you are not a successful human being first, nothing else you do matters.

We experience what we call failure when something **Shouting** or **Shoving** inside us sabotages our ability to be successful. Right from the start you need to realize that only successful thinking creates success. If you're not programmed for success, then you obviously won't be successful.

If we program ourselves to expect the worst and are afraid of less than favorable outcomes, we will seldom pursue things. If our programming includes values of growth through new experiences, perseverance and learning from experience, we will be eager to pursue things. Granted, no amount of successful thinking replaces a clear strategy for setting and achieving goals and the means for going about achieving them.

SETTING AND WORKING YOUR GOAL

First you made your Hara decision that something has got to change or that you want something more. The question still remains: What do you want? Amazingly this can be a difficult question to answer for some. If you can't answer this question, then stop reading right now until you can. You have to know with utmost precision what you are aiming for. Otherwise you might as well be looking for a needle in a haystack, at night, blindfolded, with your hands tied behind your back. When you're driving some place, you can't have a ballpark idea where you're going; you need an address, or you'll drive around endlessly until you run out of gas.

If you think you do know what you want, be sure you don't confuse "What *do* I want" with "What *should* I want?" I've come across too many people who put all of their energy into accomplishing the goals they were raised to think were important (e.g., acquiring cars, money, etc.) and end up characters in a miserable success story. Be sure the question you're asking is "What *do* I want?"

I know of many people who complain about the way their lives are and when you ask them what they want to make things better, they don't know. They put so much energy into being dissatisfied that they haven't thought for a second about what it might take to improve things. When you can answer the question, "What do I want?" answer it as specifically as possible. Then you have your goal, and you may proceed.

THINKING INSIDE OUT

After you determine what you want, you should then complete an exercise I call "Inside Out." Picture your goal in your head as clearly as a photograph. Describe, in as much detail as possible, how it looks, from every angle. Study it and build it so that you can see it, feel it and touch it. If you can't see it in great detail, you'll have a hard time recognizing it when you come upon it. Let it become as real to you as your own heartbeat so that no one can ever convince you that you're experience is unrealistic or impossible.

Then imagine that your goal isn't inside your head anymore; it is actually outside in your life. You have achieved it. Now ask yourself, "How is my life different now that I've achieved this goal? How do I feel about it or about myself?" The greater your commitment to this exercise the more powerful the result. When you do it correctly, you will be left with the experience of achieving your goal and

Please Visit www.LifeTeamStrategy.com

the belief that you have the ability to do so. Like the saying goes, seeing is believing. The only thing that remains is to take the necessary action to make your life look identical to the picture in your head. This exercise is all about setting the stage for making the reality in your head the reality of your life.

Once you've done the Inside Out exercise and know precisely where you're going, you can proceed with determining how you are going to get there. Often, not enough thought is put into a goal to gauge if it will truly create what we want for ourselves—especially if we strive for goals based on the dreams others have for us that we may not truly have for ourselves. In addition, the clearer we can see the treasures that lie in achieving the goal, the greater the incentive for reaching it. To achieve any goal you must proceed step by step: let's begin simply.

The process for accomplishing any goal can be seen as similar to the task of climbing a ladder. There is the starting point, the destination and the steps needed to get there. First you need a goal. Let's use the goal of getting dressed for work in the morning as an example. My starting point is assembling the clothes I intend to put on. What are the steps to get there? The way I do it is:

1. Underwear on
2. Shirt on
3. Pants on
4. Socks on
5. Shoes on
6. Tie on
7. Jacket on

I am dressed for work.

The steps needed to get to the goal of getting dressed are very clear cut. I know what the steps are, and I can tell when they've been completed. If you can't visualize how a goal is going to be accomplished, you can't visualize yourself accomplishing it. Writing down your objectives (i.e., the steps required to achieve your goal) helps provide you with a concrete visual of how you need to proceed, just as looking at a ladder lets you know where the next rung is as you're climbing it. Anytime you set a goal, your objectives must be clear, feasible and achievable. If your objectives aren't clear, you won't know when you've accomplished them. If they aren't feasible, meaning you don't have the means to carry them out, then

Please Visit www.LifeTeamStrategy.com

you won't be prepared to achieve them. Let's say you want to build a house. You've got the blueprints and the objectives clearly spelled out, so you know exactly what you need to do. In this case, your goal and objectives are clear. But you don't have money for the materials, so it isn't feasible. Or let's say you don't have the knowledge of construction required to build a house so it may not be achievable. Your goal can only be reached when the previous challenges are resolved.

By clearly stating what is needed at the outset, you can eliminate as many challenges as possible before you begin. You must know where you want to go, where you are at and what resources you currently have at your disposal. Then you can determine what else is required.

A very important point: You can set a goal for yourself without knowing how you're going to get there. When President Kennedy set the goal to put a man on the moon, he had no idea what it would take to accomplish it. But because his goal was so magnificent, those whose shoulders it fell upon to make it happen did whatever it took to make it real. In my opinion, every goal is feasible and achievable. The point in assessing what your resources are now is so you know what you have to go out and learn or get at the outset so you don't keep tripping over preventable obstacles along the way. If Thomas Edison can take us from candle to lightbulb and the Wright Brothers from ground to flight, then clearly your ability to create anything and everything you want is limited only by your imagination and tenacity.

PARTIALIZING

Now that you know how to structure your goal and objectives, you must address how you perceive the process of achieving the goal. Look back at the list of objectives for getting dressed. Which step do you think is the most important? Many people I've asked have told me they think the last step is the most important because it is the final one, which means they've reached their goal. My answer is different. I think that each step is as important as the others are. The only thing special about the final step or even the goal itself is that it is the last one. It is the standard you established that lets you know when you're done. By all means take time to congratulate yourself on your achievement. But remember that your goal is also the first step for your next project.

Like building a house or getting dressed, each step in the process is of equal importance in reaching the final goal. If the doctors had decided to skip something in my cancer treatment, I don't imagine it would have had the same outcome. If a step is missed or done incorrectly, the quality of the final goal is compromised. If the foundation of a house is not laid with the utmost attention because you're distracted by your eagerness to start putting up the walls, it may not be able to support the walls adequately. If the walls are not strong and sturdy, they will not support the roof. As a result of not partializing (breaking your goal down into smaller steps) and staying focused on the total completion of each objective, the house could come tumbling down.

By writing down your objectives, you have the luxury of only having to think about the current one. The list is there for your reference so you don't need to keep everything in your head that is likely to distract you.

Anyone who wishes to build a house may look at the list of objectives or the immensity of the final goal and say from a **Shouter** point of view, "Man, that's a daunting task. I don't think I can do it. Why did I ever think I could build a house?" First of all, this is failure thinking, not success thinking. Remember: Only success thinking creates success. When you sit down and partialize your goal, you must embrace only those thoughts that will help you achieve each objective. "I sure hope I don't screw this up" is not an ingredient for success. You don't make a cake with dirt in it, because dirt isn't an ingredient in successfully making a cake. All it will do is make it taste lousy and probably not bake properly, all because you added one useless ingredient. If it doesn't help you, you can't use it, so leave it where you found it.

Others might do the **Shouting** for you by saying, "You're a dreamer," "Keep your feet on the ground" or "Don't set your standards too high—you'll only be disappointed." Or even worse, "You're not smart enough for that" or "You'll never do it." When partializing your goals and picturing the ingredients necessary for achieving them, which of the previous statements will help you to achieve them? That's right—none of them. So don't add them to your formula. The idea of knowingly adding something to a cake that would ruin it seems absurd. But we often allow the words or actions of others to poison our goals and dreams and negatively affect the outcome. If you can't use it, then lose it. It's that simple.

So what are the thoughts of success? **Starter** statements like, "I will do this" or "There is a way, and I will find it." Thoughts that keep you solution focused instead of problem/obstacle focused and with success as the only outcome are the keys to victory in the game of life.

Remember, you don't pave roads with mud—you use concrete. Concrete is strong and solid and supports you as you drive toward successful completion of your journey. Using mud for paving has the same effect as using doubt, criticism

Please Visit www.LifeTeamStrategy.com

and unsuccessful thinking when setting or working toward your goal. You sink in it, you can't get good footing, you slip and fall a lot and soon you're covered in it. Now that you're covered in mud, you're so involved in it that you can no longer proceed on your journey. Instead, pave the path toward your goals with concrete as you build and support your objectives with the thoughts of success that will keep you moving forward. Thoughts such as, "This is what is required, and this is how I'm going to do it," are the thoughts of success. Or, "I may not be sure how to do it, but I'm going to find out how." You must visualize the task in your head and its accomplishment, with only success in mind. If you can't see it, you can't achieve it, because it won't appear real and you won't be able to recognize it when you get there.

Early in my high school years, my friends and I would have discussions about what we thought we'd be able to deal with if we had to. When we considered if we'd be able to handle having cancer, we all agreed we didn't think we'd be able to. I'm sure this contributed to their reaction to my diagnosis. When it comes down to it, none of us has the slightest inkling what we can withstand until we're called upon to do so. I've heard many stories of elderly grandmothers lifting cars off of grandchildren, an ability they would likely see as beyond themselves if asked hypothetically. But when it becomes necessary, guess what happens? One of the greatest human assets is our ability to rise to the occasion. Instead of questioning your ability to do anything, understand that you could if you had to or chose to.

Part of dealing with cancer meant I had to learn how to partialize. As I recovered and set my goals for how my life was to become, I had to plan day-to-day what I could do that day based on how strong I felt. The most important thing, however, is to do something. There is a simple law of physics that states that things in motion tend to stay in motion, and things at rest tend to stay at rest. So once you begin to pursue a goal, don't stop.

Another thing that can interfere with your ability to stick to the pursuit of your goal, in addition to your own negative thinking, is the criticisms you get from others. First of all, always remember that everyone is the foremost expert on their own opinion, especially when they mistake it for fact. Some of the biggest lies and misconceptions are delivered with utmost confidence. If someone tries to talk you out of seeking a goal, find out for yourself if his or her reasoning is correct. Even if it is, if you want your goal bad enough, determine what you can do to succeed in spite of the new information. Every time Thomas Edison found that a particular filament wouldn't work, he used another. After 10,000 experiments he found the one that worked and successfully invented the lightbulb. He wanted it bad enough, and he refused to give up. Those who may have encouraged him to quit were all wrong. I can't tell you how many times I've heard the phrase, "Trust me, it isn't going to work." If everybody believed that when it was told to them, we'd still be lighting our houses by candle.

Your own determination may be a threat to others if you're attempting something they were unable or too afraid to do themselves. If you succeed, you rob them of their excuses, which is psychologically dangerous for them. Be wary of how much of their own self-doubt is being flung at you through their comments. If the person you're talking to is a **Shover** you tend to compete with, they'll likely employ some **Shouting** criticism aimed at preventing you from becoming more successful than them. Whatever their motivation, your motivation needs to remain the same: success, success, success, whether it is in your career, family, love or life in general. Investing your energy in developing the kind of thinking and skills needed to accomplish the goals you set for yourself is not just an investment in success. It is first and foremost an investment in yourself.

Assembling the Puzzle

Whatever education or skills you acquire as you travel through this life, you are your primary instrument. It is you who utilizes your education and you who practices these skills. In addition to acquiring knowledge, you must actively refine yourself. Make yourself as sharp and effective a tool as you can be. A blunt saw doesn't cut very well.

We are not only our own primary **Starter** in life; we can also be our own primary **Shover** or **Shouter** as well. When it comes time to set out to make our way in life, it is our own programming, thoughts, doubts and all that destructive criticism that we tell ourselves that is responsible for holding us back. If an arrow is going to fly straight and hit its target, it must have a smooth shaft, a straight tail and a sharpened point. Otherwise, it could curve in flight and miss the target. That is why it is so important in shaping and refining ourselves that our make up keeps us flying straight and prevents us from losing track of our target. To refine yourself for success, make sure your destination is always clear and you are prepared to fly right toward your target.

Now let's continue talking about achieving our goals. You know about partializing and thinking for success, but you also need to know how to stay that way. Spending a lot of time looking at the overall goal can cause anxiety because of the size of the task. For example, don't think about the overall goal of building a house; the house is only the endpoint of having achieved the other steps properly. Your first step may be to cut some lumber (not a daunting task) or to hammer some boards together (not daunting either). Eventually you may have to lay some tile. As you complete each step, the end result—your goal of building a house—will happen on its own. You simply move to the next objective after the previous one is completed. Of course, your eye might glance at the final goal once in a while. But use your list of objectives to keep you focused on the immediate task.

Now you know how important your programming and ability to partialize can be. Reprogramming ourselves to think successfully can be difficult and quite challenging. For some, partializing on paper is one thing, but being able to stay that way in your mind is another story. However, as you begin practicing the Immediacy Skill that will be introduced later you will see how easily you can reprogram yourself. First here's an analogy to help further clarify the value and power of partializing.

Think of every goal you aspire to as a completed puzzle. The steps to achieve it require that the pieces be placed in the correct order. Of course, the puzzle may appear vast depending on the size of the goal. Its apparent complexity can be overwhelming. However, if you look at the puzzle more closely, what do you see? A series of small, interconnected, unintimidating pieces that comprise the puzzle. You can place each piece in the palm of your hand and observe its modesty. Each solitary piece of the vast puzzle is so minute and simple. It poses no threat to you at all. Now you are no longer focused on the magnitude of the puzzle or the goal. You realize that all that is required of you is to assemble it piece by piece, step by step, in order to reach the final goal.

As the puzzle is assembled one piece at a time, life is constructed one moment at a time, and every challenge arises little by little. Life is a unique compilation of pieces that are not all available at the outset. Often you must complete one task before the next one reveals itself. When opportunities present themselves, the challenge then lies in choosing the correct one. The clearer your goal, the easier it should be to see which opportunity will lead you there.

Choosing incorrectly can leave you with a piece that doesn't fit. Such decisions can cause pain in life, as a hole is now left where the correct piece is desperately needed. It is hard to say when the correct piece will present itself again. And although each piece of the puzzle is different, it is complementary to the previous piece and all others as well. Though small in size, it assists in supporting the entire design. So our decisions and placement are very important, no matter how small a decision it seems to be.

Please Visit www.LifeTeamStrategy.com

This puzzle is never completed in one's lifetime, as our challenges are ongoing. Each moment provides us with an opportunity to improve upon the moment before. Only by being fully aware and focused as the puzzle is constructed can we know which piece will best complement the others. In doing so, the chances are very good that each decision made will be the correct one. The lives we construct will be strong. The regrets in our minds will be none.

4

Taking Life the Only Way It Comes

We've all heard the saying, "Take life one moment at a time," like this is an option. Of course you have to take life one moment at a time—that's the only way it comes. No matter how hasty our schedule or how limited our patience, life moves at the same rate.

I discovered the profound value of one moment during my stint in isolation during chemo. I noticed the large face of the clock that was hanging on the wall across from me. The room was absolutely silent, and the ticking of the clock was deafening. As I followed the rhythm of the clock, I noticed that it seemed to synchronize with the beating of my own heart. Counting the moments of my life. It was from this that I came to realize that life occurs in moments. It didn't happen in minutes, hours or days. I understood that each heartbeat was the beginning and end of each opportunity in my life. The more I focused on my heartbeat, the rhythm of the clock and each and every moment, the more I realized a greater sense of peace. I became less inclined to anticipate and become anxious about a future that didn't exist or to obsess about the pains from my past. This experience was the beginning of moment-to-moment living for me. Now I will teach you how to begin to do the same.

MOMENT TO MOMENT

Find a clock with a second hand on it. Watch the second hand for a minute or so. Tick, tick, tick. It progresses smoothly, no haste, no impatience. It proceeds in a constant rhythm. Now consider some of the expressions we use to describe time: "time seems to be dragging along," "time flies," "running out of time," "wasted time." Time doesn't drag or fly, it's steady. Nor can we waste it or run out of it; it is infinite. What changes is our awareness, and that's something that can be wasted. So let's see if we can start to view time differently, more closely to how it actually is.

THE MOMENT HAND

From this moment on, every time you see a clock do not view this moving arm as a second hand. Instead, refer to it as a moment hand. Although the clock face is typically segmented as though to imply that time is broken up in some way, you can see that the second hand is not inhibited, its progress not impeded. Our perception of time, however, has always been an impediment to us and a source of great stress. There seems to never be enough of it.

In actuality, time is a manmade concept; it isn't what we perceive it to be. Neither time, nor life, occurs in seconds, hours or days. Life occurs in moments—one moment at a time, strung together like pearls on a necklace. Hence the designation of the moment hand on the clock. I find this to be a more accurate designation of the actual quality of time. The clock is a tangible representation of the actual moment-to-moment speed of life.

With this new perception of time as an unlimited commodity, there is always enough, so much so that it loses its constrictive quality. It's not in a rush, so why should we be? Even in human's attempt to design an instrument to master the length of a day, he or she was uncontrollably bound by the moment-to-moment movement of life. Clocks surround you all day long. When you apply pressure to yourself to move faster than the speed of life, you will inevitably burn yourself out with stress. All because you tried to reach for something clearly out of your grasp. The discomfort of stress is like a pulled muscle that results from trying to move faster than the speed of life—from trying to carry a burden or responsibility that is beyond us to carry.

From now on a clock need not only be a measure of this thing we call time. It can also serve as a reminder to reorient and calm yourself. You can begin by taking a minute to watch the moment hand and return your awareness to the moment-to-moment speed of life—the actual pace of things rather than the anxiety-building speed we are encouraged to live at. This way a clock is transformed from an object that compels us to hurry to a reminder to calm and pace ourselves.

Please Visit www.LifeTeamStrategy.com

Minding the Breath, Minding the Hara

Moment-to-moment living cannot be embraced if you only understand it conceptually. You have to feel it if you're going to practice it. The best way I've found to experience the moment is in the experience I first had in the hospital when I experienced the breath moving in and out of my body, moment to moment. As I refined this practice, I found it to be a powerful way to center my mind and tap into the power of my Hara. Through this exercise I learned to embrace change and increase my ability to remain mentally alert, focused and calm. An essential skill to functioning fully in any circumstance is knowing how to mind your breath.

First I would suggest finding a place to sit down. A comfortable chair will do, one where your feet lie flat on the ground and the back of your thighs rest flat on the chair. You're looking for a spot where you can sit comfortably and sit straight up without the need to constantly readjust yourself. Your hands should be resting comfortably on your lap but close to your abdomen. If they are too far out your shoulders will round forward and you will no longer be sitting up straight.

Now, point your face straight ahead but cast your eyes gently down about two-thirds of the way. Your eyes should be open, but they shouldn't be focusing on anything. You should be concerned only with feeling your breath, not looking at anything. You may want to face a blank wall so your eyes won't be inclined to wander. Next, relax your shoulders and then the rest of your body. You only want enough tension to maintain your posture. You must be relaxed to practice calmness but not so relaxed that you feel drowsy. You're training your mind for alertness and focus, not sloth.

Once your posture is stable, just begin to feel your breathing. Breathe in and out through your nose, and allow your breaths to naturally become deep. This is not lung breathing we're talking about; you should be feeling your abdomen rise and fall. You are breathing from your Hara for this exercise. Allow your Hara to become filled with air.

You may be tempted to force yourself to breathe deeper but don't. You're body naturally breathes more deeply when it is calm. So just allow the breathing to happen on its own, and you will gradually feel it deepen. Relax your abdomen as you breathe so that your diaphragm can easily expand and your lungs can fill completely. The more relaxed the abdomen, the deeper the breath.

Lastly, the manner in which you mind or mentally watch your breath is essential. As I said before, your breathing is happening spontaneously, and you are not manipulating it in any way. The abdomen rises, and the abdomen falls. The

Please Visit www.LifeTeamStrategy.com

breath moves in, the breath moves out. Watch each inhalation, and each exhalation. Observe moment to moment.

This is the most important point for this exercise, so pay attention. If it is your desire to learn to live from your Hara, then you must master minding the breath as it falls into your Hara. As you are minding your breath, you are minding your center. Therefore, your mind becomes centered. There is nothing clearer and more focused than a centered mind, so practice this diligently. With enough practice, minding your breath will be all that is required to center your mind and work from your Hara.

As you practice minding the breath, you may begin to experience thoughts running through your mind, such as everything you have to do today. This is common because when your mind is clear, anything can fly in to try and take your mind away. So you need to practice taking your mind back. When you notice that you've become distracted, all you need to do is acknowledge that fact and return to minding your breath. Eventually, with much practice, the thoughts that enter won't even catch your attention; they will just enter and leave.

In doing this you are practicing keeping your mind focused on exactly what you're doing at this moment. When a thought of something else rushes in, you're simply putting it aside and getting back to what you're doing. Eventually, this ability will work its way into every activity in your life so that you'll be able to focus intensely with little or no distraction.

You should practice this exercise for no less than five minutes at a time, as it may take a bit for your mind and breath to become calm. Half an hour or more at a time is ideal. Don't be upset with yourself if you aren't able to perfect this technique right away. Initially your mind can be like a racehorse that was just let out of the gate. It may take time for it to slow down. Be diligent and patient. Your mind will become more and more trainable, but you must practice and practice often.

Through this practice you learn not to become distracted by things that are not related to what you're doing. You learn to stay on task by concentrating precisely on what's happening in this moment. No matter how busy the environment is around you, you are concerned with where you're at in that situation and tending to it. This is a powerful tool. Once your mind is trained for this, you can walk into chaos and remain calm. After all, this practice teaches you not to seek control in the moment or manipulate your breath or the thoughts racing through your mind but just watch them and let them be. You look to control yourself instead. Walking through a chaotic office or school day is no different. Control yourself, watch the situation, understand it and then act according to your two responsibilities.

Let's continue exploring just how relevant this practice is in everyday life. We often speak in terms of the past or the future as if these were tangible entities. In actuality, the past is gone—done, finished. The past is done with us whether or not we are done with the past. All we have to work with now are the present consequences and present opportunities. After experiencing unforeseen consequences I often hear people say, "I should've done this, or I could've done that." In essence, putting their mental energy on a desire to make a repair of the past that can't be made. This gets you nowhere. Instead, work with what you have, not with what is gone. The results are your building blocks.

The other side of this coin is the future, which is fantasy. The future is nothing but a projection—a story we construct based upon our own ideals about what we wish things to be. You can't do anything there either. I'm not saying it's bad to set goals for ourselves or to think about those goals. Goals are essential. But where is the work done to achieve these goals? Right here, right now, in the present.

When running a marathon, the consideration of running 26 miles can be overwhelming and even discouraging. The end point is not the only point but one of many. Your task lies in tending to each step, or each moment, of the process literally. As your awareness lies with each step, your task becomes the process as opposed to a far-off destination. Just as the ocean begins with a single drop of water, any seemingly overwhelming task can become as simple and manageable. Sitting and watching your breath for half an hour or more may seem difficult, but your actual task is watching a single breath. If you keep doing that, before you know it half an hour has passed. Minding the breath can be difficult to master, but it is one of the best ways for mastering the Hara mindset.

Calming your mind can be difficult, but so is calming the body and minimizing the stress it carries. The key to beginning to relieve stress and tension in your life is to first know that you are experiencing them. I am a practitioner of the Japanese healing art called Shiatsu, which uses pressure points on the body to help resolve many ailments, including tension brought on by stress. Often as I work on someone who claims to be relaxed, I find several points on his or her body that are solid balls of tension. These points feel like tight knots, and when I press on them the person yells in pain. In spite of how obviously tense these people are, they either lack the self-awareness to realize it or they are tense and stressed as a matter of routine and have just become psychologically desensitized to its presence in their lives and bodies.

But as any physician will tell you, whether you are aware of the stress you have in your life or not, enduring it long term without buffering it in some way can have damaging consequences, like ulcers, heart disease or a weakening of the immune system to name a few. Minding the breathing as you've just learned is wonderful for calming the mind, which of course will gradually calm the body. But there are other exercises that can calm the body more quickly and deeply. These techniques will increase your awareness of your body as readily as minding the breath increases your awareness of your mind. It stands to reason that the more aware you are of your body, the more quickly you will notice tension beginning to build so you can begin preventing it from doing so. As you first learn these exercises, they may seem incredibly detailed and lengthy. But once you're familiar with them and become proficient, they may take no more than a few minutes to complete.

EXTERNAL BODY SCAN

The first technique, called the External Body Scan, is very effective for unscrewing the tension from your body. The second is the Internal Body Scan, which is a bit more difficult but very important as our insides often suffer greater damage from stress than our outsides. We will start with the External Body Scan.

This technique is to assist you in determining the spots on your body where you store stress. Although the instructions move quickly, make sure you spend as much time with each area as necessary. After all, we each distribute stress differently, and one area may require more attention than another.

Begin by finding a quiet place to lie down. It needs to be quiet so you can concentrate, and you need to be able to lie flat on your back with your arms at your side. Once you are lying down, close your eyes and relax as much as possible. Start minding your breath so your breathing becomes deep. Once you have been breathing deep for a minute or two, begin to scan your body.

Direct your attention to the top of your head. Focus on it as though the rest of your body doesn't exist. Concentrate on relaxing the top of your head and letting the tension dissolve, releasing the muscles. You can also use your exhalation, relaxing that part of your body as you breath out. It's like you're exhaling your tension. Sometimes its helpful to flex the muscles in question and then release them completely, but I find it more useful to just relax the muscles from the point they are at.

Please Visit www.LifeTeamStrategy.com

Next move your attention to your forehead; when it is relaxed, move to your nose, then your cheeks, your ears and then your jaw. It's perfectly fine if your mouth falls open from relaxing your jaw—don't feel you have to close it. Now relax the back of your head, and this will complete the relaxation of the muscles in your head and face. Before moving on, gradually but somewhat quickly move your attention through all of the areas of your head and face one more time to make sure none of them have tensed up again. If they have, simply repeat the process as before to release them. When you're head and face are completely relaxed you can move on.

Next, move to the back of the neck, and slowly feel the tension releasing from the left side followed by the right. As you move below the head, you will relax things from one side to the other, so choose which side you are going to relax first and stay with that side consistently. Now continue relaxing your neck. Relax the sides of the neck and then the front.

From the front of your neck, slowly draw your attention out along one of your shoulders and relax the area between your neck and shoulder one side at a time. Then relax each shoulder. After your shoulders are completely relaxed, begin moving your attention down your upper arm. Relax the back of your upper arm and then the front. Next relax your elbow. Now begin relaxing your lower arm. Then relax your wrist followed by the back of your hand and the palm of your hand. Finally, relax each finger one at a time. Scan this arm one more time to make sure none of the muscles have tensed again, and then complete the same process with the other arm. When both arms are relaxed, move to your upper chest.

Bring your attention back to the front of your neck, and slowly relax the pectoral/breast area of your upper chest. Focus on each muscle of the front of your chest individually and thoroughly. Then relax each side of your chest (the area that would be covered if you put your arms against your sides). Next draw your attention to your abdomen, and relax it as deeply as you can. Now scan your chest and abdomen again before moving on.

Move your attention to the back of your neck, and then focus on the area between your shoulder blades. Then relax one shoulder blade at a time. Now move your attention slowly down your spine, and relax it as you go (only your spine, not the back muscles). Once this is done, return your focus to one of your shoulder blades, then gradually move your attention down that side of your back, relaxing the muscles as you go. Once reaching the top of the buttock on that side, start over with the other side. After finishing the back the first time, relax it again, but this time relax both sides simultaneously. Some people find it difficult to get

Please Visit www.LifeTeamStrategy.com

the back to relax one side at a time, so this can be a helpful way to finish this part of the body.

Next you want to relax your buttocks, then one leg at a time. Slowly relax the back of your upper leg, then the front, then relax your knee. When finished with that, you want to relax your lower leg, front and back, and the bottom of the foot followed by the top. Like the fingers, relax each toe one at a time. Then do the same with the other leg. If you like, you can quickly scan your body from head to toe once more to smooth everything out.

Now that you've scanned the outside of your body, you've probably discovered those parts of your body that seemed unusually tense. Using this exercise to tune into each part of your body is intended to make you more aware of how your body feels in a relaxed state. This way when tension begins to build you are quickly aware of it and can mentally isolate that area and begin to relax it. In the long run, you'll no longer have those days where you come home with a stiff neck from having saved that tension until the end of the day; instead you'll start working on relieving the stress right away.

I wouldn't recommend working on the internal body scan until you're familiar with the external one. It helps to have well-developed concentration, relaxation and visualization skills before moving on.

INTERNAL BODY SCAN

The internal body scan is designed to help you to release the internal tension of your body. Think of your body's tension as a volcano. Deep below the surface you have the pressure building, and eventually it surfaces in knots in your neck muscles or lower back pain. So, to calm the volcano, you need to go deeper. We started with the external body scan because those feelings of tension are more evident.

The internal body scan requires more imagination. You have to mentally release the tension inside you. Some of it is easy to locate. All you need to do is find a place on your body that feels uncomfortable or painful. If you can't attribute pain or discomfort to an injury and have otherwise ruled out a medical explanation for it, then you're left with stress as a cause. In addition, your own dislike of the presence of pain can intensify your experience of it. In order to relieve that pain you can use the following process.

It is probably a good idea to complete the external body scan before beginning the internal scan. This way your mind is primed for deliberately bringing about relaxation in the body. Find a quiet place, and assume a comfortable position. Bring your awareness into that area of your body that's causing you discomfort; you may even want to place your hand over the area if it helps you to focus. Next, ask yourself, "If this pain or discomfort could speak, what would it say?" Begin to speak out loud on your pain's behalf; you may be surprised by what it has to say. I have often found my lower back pain to be in response to nervousness. So I do this exercise and verbalize my nervousness, and I talk for as long as it takes. But remember, in order to relieve the nervousness or whatever feeling you're currently experiencing, you have to replace it with reassurance. Statements like, "It can be scary to do _____, but I know I have it in me to do it, and I'm going to do well no matter what the outcome." In this way you're not denying your frustration, you acknowledge it, but you're also acknowledging your own competence. It's kind of like giving yourself a mental hug. There are still deeper tensions we may not be as aware of, however. Here's how we get at them.

Since you've just completed the external body scan, you should already be on your back and well relaxed. To assist you in concentrating on each organ as you tend to it, you're going to use one of your hands. Remember that you're not supposed to feel your organ relaxing; this exercise requires your imagination and is designed more for you to just be compassionate toward yourself and become more aware of those parts of your body where stress and tension can cause harm. This exercise is a way for you to cultivate peace in your body.

Allow your breathing to become deep as you proceed. Start with the organ whose location is not difficult to find. Take your hand, and place it on the center of your upper chest over your heart. In the previous exercise your mind focused on the surface of the body; now your mind needs to focus deeper. Begin by focusing your mind on the skin beneath the surface of your hand. Then slowly allow your mind to sink into your body about three inches until you can picture yourself inside the organ in question. In this case, feel yourself inside your beating heart, and picture it pumping life-giving blood throughout your body. Feel it contract, imagine its strength.

If emotions are weighing heavily on your heart, then allow them to beat to the surface, because this is the heart's time to be cared for. Feel the emotion reach through the skin on your chest and through your hand where it disperses in the air. You can even imagine it emerging under your hand as a bubble, and simply move your hand to release it. Then place your hand back against your heart and speak words of comfort to it. This may not make the emotions or the feelings go away completely, but it should at least help you tap into them.

Please Visit www.LifeTeamStrategy.com

Now slide your hand straight down slowly until your thumb rests just below the bottom of the sternum, which is the bone your hand was just sliding down. At this point your hand is resting on a portion of your liver. Your liver is responsible for cleaning the refuse and many of the poisons from your body. Again, begin with your attention on the skin beneath your hand. Then allow your mind to sink into your liver. Picture your liver, and be grateful for its protection of the rest of your body. Imagine how it is filtering the poison from your blood and how important it is for you to minimize its workload through your own habits. Place your mind inside your liver, and mentally push your image of the toxins in your blood through your liver and then out.

Next move your hand to the left until it is on your lower ribcage. Your hand is now resting on part of your stomach. This is one of the few internal organs besides the heart and lungs that you can actually feel working, especially when it is upset. As your hand rests upon it and your mind sinks into it, imagine it calming down. Picture it relaxing as you would a muscle. Spend a little time concentrating on it and encouraging it to function well. Rest your mind inside it as you would rest it if you were laying your head on a pillow. Picture your stomach as soft, without tension.

Now place your hand over your belly button. You're now in the general location of your intestines, which can become quite upset and loose when you're under stress. As your hand rests over your abdomen, imagine your intestines moving strongly and smoothly. Move your mind into them. Feel how they are strong but relaxed. They are healthy and keeping themselves cleansed. Rubbing your abdomen in a clockwise fashion as you are picturing your intestines can help this image. Allow your mind to follow beneath your hand as it moves in a circle across your belly, and mentally work to push the toxins through and out.

Lastly, return your hand to the position over your navel. This time focus on your abdomen as it rises and falls. Sink your attention into your Hara. Through this motion you will focus on your lungs. Feel your abdomen rise as your breath becomes deeper. Feel your abdomen fall as your lungs release the old stale air from your body. Allow your awareness to be filled with each inhalation and exhalation as your lungs fill your body with the life-giving oxygen you need. Feel how clear and strong your lungs are. Feel how much more alive you become with each breath.

You may also spend some time minding your breath at the end of this exercise. This is a great opportunity to strengthen your Hara and your awareness of it since you are so relaxed and better able to concentrate.

Please Visit www.LifeTeamStrategy.com

Spend as much time on each organ as is necessary for your image of its proper functioning to become clear. This is not to say that your imagery will improve its functioning, but it should improve your awareness of its function and thus your treatment of yourself.

Now lay your hand back at your side and relax for a few minutes. Clearly we did not cover every organ of the body, but we did cover the major ones. Again, the idea here is increased awareness of where stress can be stored in the body. The more you see it coming and building, the better you will be at heading it off.

Minding the breath and the external and internal body scans are profound methods for training your mind to live moment to moment and for experiencing how your body and mind are being affected in each moment. After all, the moment is where life occurs and where you have the greatest opportunity to be most effective in life. Now that you can live in the moment while relaxing, let's learn how to do it on the move.

5

Immediacy

I will now teach you a less complicated way of mastering the moment until you become comfortable with the minding the breath exercise. The "Immediacy Skill," although easier to grasp, is made more powerful when backed with the abilities cultivated while minding the breath. So this is not an either or kind of thing; you must practice and use both.

One added benefit of this new technique is that you are not in a resting state while you practice the immediacy skill. You are actively going about your everyday life. Keep in mind that this skill helps your mind touch only the surface of moment-to-moment living because it employs your thoughts to master the moment. Hopefully you discovered that the minding the breath exercise allows you to get a richer, fuller experience of the moment.

As with minding the breath, the immediacy skill enables you to focus on precisely what you're doing now. This allows you to be more productive and efficient because you are difficult to distract. I have found that the fewer distractions people indulge in, internal or external, the clearer their perceptions are of exactly what needs to be done, both in the short term and long term. In order to be effective long term, you must be effective short term, which means you must be effective every single moment. Toward that end you must master immediacy, which is what this skill is all about.

The immediacy skill leads to increased focus and reduction of stress even in the most adverse situations. As I mentioned, this skill is actually part of the process of the activity you're engaged in. What you're doing actually helps you to relax and focus.

Those who have had the opportunity to learn and use this skill have expressed a significant reduction in the stress of their everyday lives. They describe how they experience an increased ability to focus, which results in greater productivity both at work and in their private lives. There is no reason why you shouldn't reap the same benefits. Now it is time for you to begin learning and applying the immediacy skill.

THE IMMEDIACY SKILL

As you embrace the responsibility for who you are and what you do, you need to hone in on operating in the present. At any given time of the day, as you are pursuing any goal, you may find yourself getting carried away with thoughts about your task. This brings us to:

Rule #1: Don't lose track of your head.

In other words, keep your head and your body in the same place—in the present. Don't let your mind spend too much time in the future because your body is always in the present. Likewise, don't let your mind dwell in the past while your body is in the present. This is how we experientially tear ourselves in half. Our mind is drudging up a previous experience while the body is having the present one.

We can become "headless" when we begin to spin stories in our head about all of the things that might happen if the responsibility isn't carried out or if the goal isn't achieved. We begin "what-ifing" every decision we make. "What if I make the same mistake as last time?" "What if it isn't as good as last time?" "What if I fail?" "What if others don't like it?" How many of the "what-ifs" involve the potential of uncontrollable factors getting in our way? "What-ifing" and supposing are the fertilizers for anxiety. You can "what-if" yourself to the point of inaction by robbing yourself of the energy you could otherwise use to take action. "What-ifs" have nothing to do with the "what is" of your task. Your thoughts need to focus on what you can do to achieve success, not on the hypothetical threats to it that you can't control. What you're doing is the reality, and it's time to realize that the uncontrollables take care of themselves, whether we fret about them or not. The sun comes up whether we worry about it or not. Whether we wake up at all each day sets the stage for our next move. All we can control are our two responsibilities—everything else is out of our hands.

As we can often get preoccupied with the uncontrollables, it is our responsibility to bring our mind back to what it is actually doing, since that's its only responsibility. Now that we know we can only have full control over who we are and what we do and that the place we can maximize them is in the present, now is the time to learn how this is done. Start simple.

Every morning you wake up and go through a ritual that prepares you for the day. When I was sick this was simple because what was simple was all I could do. Since I felt I couldn't plan for much else, I simply concentrated on enjoying what I was doing, and this became a profoundly valuable awareness skill.

So as you prepare for your day, at any given point you may notice your mind begin to spin in great detail about every little thing that must be accomplished that day. I have to go here and do this, then after that, and on and on. But soon you realize that this spinning has nothing to do with what you're doing at the time. So bring your mind back to the present by telling yourself what you're actually doing. If you're combing your hair when your mind starts spinning, tell yourself silently, "I'm combing my hair." Keep telling yourself that until that's all your mind is doing. If you're eating your breakfast, say to yourself, "I'm eating breakfast." Or even more immediate "I'm lifting the spoon." After a while you can focus simply on the action: combing, eating, lifting, gradually training your body and mind to concentrate on the immediate task with your undivided attention. This is how you keep your head and body in the present together. In doing so you have just accomplished immediacy or mindfulness, which is a deliberate, conscious involvement in the present. Before long you won't have to think about doing this—it will become automatic, and you will become naturally focused.

Granted, the spinning in your head may revolve around important tasks, but they are irrelevant until the conditions arise under which they can be accomplished. Having to complete a task at work is hardly doable or even relevant while your current task is brushing your teeth. When you get to work, whatever you're doing then is your task; everything at home is finished and gone so now you can concentrate on work. "I'm signing this document," or "I'm dialing the phone." You'll be presently surprised at how effective this is. You learn not how to put in an eight-hour day but concentrated moments of time. Which do you think is easier and less stressful to do?

Rule #2: Get off the time machine.

This rule is similar to Rule #1 and is offered more as an easier way to conceptualize this mental activity now that you've received some explanation. In other words, stop running to the future that isn't here yet and stop shouldering a past that can't be revisited or fixed. This mental ping-pong game will keep you tripping over the present but seldom stopping there.

Please Visit www.LifeTeamStrategy.com

Another thing you can do to get off the time machine is to ask yourself a question whenever you start to feel anxious. Anxiety is rooted in anticipation of past discomforts returning or an uncertain future approaching. When this occurs, ask yourself, where am I? Then make the answer as immediate as possible (e.g., I'm lying in bed, I'm sitting in a chair, I'm standing, I'm breathing), all of which are stress-free activities and not anxiety-producing. Even if you're at work, (e.g., I'm sitting at my desk, or the less stressful, I'm just sitting), embrace the immediacy until your thinking is consumed with the present and the anxiety falls away. Once you have reestablished yourself in the present in a calm activity, then a calm, focused, present-minded state is the place from where you proceed when you begin your next activity. It can be this way all the time as long as you practice this skill. The more immediate and the more focused you are, the less the temptations of the time machine will distract you. This is a powerful way to unscrew yourself when you get caught up in internal **Shouting** that results in anxiety.

The immediacy skill is especially useful when you're trying to fall asleep but can't keep your mind from racing. Keep telling yourself, "I'm lying down," "I'm resting" or "I'm just breathing.," It has the same effect as counting sheep. You can even practice minding your breath. By keeping your mind occupied, you no longer focus on the thoughts causing your mind to race. The phrase you repeat to yourself does not produce stress, so you can't help but relax more and more until you're asleep. After a while you will likely find that when you lie down for the night, your brain will just stop spinning and you will fall asleep quicker because you've trained it to do that. Neat, huh?

This is only one of many small ways you can learn to take back control. Your sense of personal control increases when you take control where you have it. Your sense of a loss of control comes from stressing over things you wouldn't have control over whether you stressed about them or not. So take them out of the equation. Keep your energy where it can be of use. You will see your stress decrease and your confidence and sense of self-efficacy increase.

After a while, bringing yourself back to what you're actually doing will teach you to automatically assess what you can and can't do in any given moment. This is because you're paying attention to the needs of the present task instead of chasing expectations and uncontrollables. Once that is assessed, any factors beyond that are not brought into consideration, and there is no room for useless stress over the situation. You will learn to determine what you can do and concentrate your energy on doing it, with complete focus and confidence.

Please Visit www.LifeTeamStrategy.com

BE LIKE WATER

I want to close this chapter with one more image to sear the values of flexibility, spontaneity and the ability to maximize who you are and what you do. I believe the greatest example of the power of these values lies in the example set by the most abundant substance on this planet: water. We human beings are at least 65% water. It is time we started acting like it.

If you watch the behavior of water, you will better understand how to be like water. When poured into a glass, water becomes the glass. When poured into a pitcher, water becomes the pitcher. It is formless and shapeless, adjusting easily to any situation. It can be liquid, ice or steam, whatever is required of it in response to environmental demands. It traverses all obstacles or wears them down with patience and perseverance. It bathes, nourishes and supports all of life, all the while adjusting to the requirements of each moment without losing its essential character. Be like water, and you'll be successful in handling every situation. All of the potential you possess comes from within you. So much of you is already made of water, so use what you've got. Do all you can, that's all you can do. Give all you can, that's all you can give. Give everything you have, because you have everything to give. Be like water.

6

Living the Cure

Your Hara decision has been made. You have been minding your breath and tapping into the boundless energy, focus and confidence that comes from doing everything from a state of balance and a strong center. Now it is time to bump it up a notch. Your cauldron of conviction and determination is gurgling—now it's time to make it boil.

If you truly want to be balanced in life and unscrew your thinking, then you must proceed without excuses. Success begins when excuses end. Excuses are the same as placing blame. If you fall short of your goal, your first question isn't "Who's fault is it?" or "What did I do wrong?" Ask only, "How can it be done differently?" No matter how many times circumstances frustrate you, you must be careful not to fall into the black hole of victimhood. This is the **Shouting** self-absorbed pity party we throw for ourselves when times are tough. I fell into it when I was sick, and I realized the toll it took.

THE BLACK HOLE OF VICTIMHOOD

What I refer to as the black hole of victimhood is the mental process we go through when something happens to us that makes us sad or feel sorry for ourselves. We begin to focus on our bad feelings, and thus our thoughts become negative as well. "I feel so sad. I'm so depressed. Nobody likes me." This kind of negative self-indulgence can, and often does, become all-consuming.

A black hole to the best of my knowledge is created by an object whose gravitational pull is so incredible that is sucks everything into itself—not even light can escape it. The role of the victim accomplishes the same goal: It effectively devours the light of hope and leaves only darkness. Victim thinking is Olympic class **Shouting** and one of the biggest cognitive cancers there is. It dominates your entire life with powerlessness and hopelessness. When you are in an unfavorable situation and you focus on what you don't like about it at the exclusion of any other thoughts, this mindset begins to consume you. Then you begin to attract greater negativity toward yourself because this is what your mind is focused on. If you think negative, then negative is all you will ever see.

If you are unsatisfied with any part of your life, there is one solution: Get off your butt and change it. If you plant a garden in which the seeds are present to grow the sweetest vegetables the world has ever known, and then you spend all of your time watering and fertilizing the weeds, then what will grow? The victim mentality accentuates the negative. The more you water the weeds, the more choked off the vegetables become.

No matter how severe our circumstances are or how traumatic an event may have been to us, the effect of the actual event never compares to how much **Shouting** we victimize ourselves with afterward. That's why control must be taken back immediately. You must separate yourself from those factors that have nothing to do with you so that you don't become obsessed with and take mental ownership of them and get caught in the black hole.

Your energy must be focused on growth not stagnation. Focus on gain not loss. I have spoken to many people who seem to be wallowing in their own misery like a pig in the mud. They are covered in it and can't see it. One of them even argued with me and said, "Sometimes you just have to let people feel bad." I thought this was some of the worst advice I'd ever heard. To me this is like standing in a burning house and making no effort to leave it because you feel entitled to burn. Before long the house will be destroyed and you along with it. If you are caught up in a destructive process, you have to get out. One might argue that people will come around in their own time. I don't agree with the rock-bottom philosophy of intervention any more than I think you should allow a house to burn down to its foundation before you try and rescue the people inside. Wallowing in your own self-pity is like riding an exercise bike: It uses up a lot of energy and gives you something to occupy your time, but it doesn't get you anywhere.

You need to begin to get out of the victim role the moment you find yourself in it. A person's own time varies when it comes to completing the journey, but at least get them on the path. The victor in you is the only thing that can save the victim in you. Remember that your circumstances are never bigger than you are. As I said before, if you want to change something, you must replace it. So here is a cure for victim thinking.

Please Visit www.LifeTeamStrategy.com

A Cure for Victim Thinking

The most important thing to realize is that we are often victimized more by the words and thoughts we use to describe an event than the actual event. To start with, we need to exchange verbs. We typically use words to describe our feelings like "scared," "frightened," "depressed," "trapped," "overwhelmed," "confused," "frustrated," etc. If you notice the common attribute of these words is that they all end in "ed." Using words like the ones above that end in "ed" is often referred to as "hidden victim language" (Canfield, 2000). It creates the impression in our minds that something was done to us; something scared us, overwhelmed us or made us feel trapped. This is the external locus of control we discussed earlier. What really happened was we indulged in some **Shouting** and did these things to ourselves. To fully understand this, let's rewrite the "ed" words so that they end in "ing."

Remember the idea here is to take back responsibility for yourself by turning **Shouting** into **Starting**. So instead of being "scared" by something else, you're actually "scaring" yourself as well as "frightening," "depressing," "trapping," "overwhelming," "confusing," and "frustrating" yourself. These feelings are the results of the thoughts you use to describe an experience to yourself. Some people expend a lot of energy depressing themselves by focusing on what they think is wrong and punishing themselves for it. Get the idea? When you realize that these experiences are your own creation, you can choose not to create them or at the very least to create them differently.

Use the same techniques you learned with the internal body scan and the immediacy skill: Realize that you're scaring or depressing yourself, and show compassion for yourself, then recognize where you actually are and what you're actually doing. By simply changing the ending of such victim words from "ed" to "ing" you change your perception from blame to responsibility and from **Shouter** to **Starter**. This will help you separate the event from the response until you eventually train yourself to create a powerful response instead of a victimizing response. By recognizing the power you have, you begin to stand as a victor in all circumstances and retire the victim.

Now You Know

Throughout this book you've received some pretty powerful tools to allow you to become more successful in life by ridding yourself of the cancerous cognitive

Please Visit www.LifeTeamStrategy.com

tumors that steal your productive energies. But success isn't just a series of accomplishments or positive thoughts. It is an attitude, a mindset that informs your actions. Successful people are made not born. If a computer isn't programmed to accomplish the tasks you want it to, it simply won't. The same goes for you. If you want to be successful you have to be programmed for it. For **Starters**, you know the two responsibilities that will truly allow you to make a difference in your own life and the lives of others solely because you have complete control in how they're carried out.

You can now begin to use time as a sail instead of an anchor. It frees you by reminding you to relax and pace yourself. Time is a continuum and finding where we landed on it makes as much sense as spending billions of dollars trying to find the corners of the universe. Realizing where you aren't doesn't help you accomplish anything.

The Immediacy Skill taught you that the only place you can do your best is in the task before you. If you're going to build a house, your mind has to be on the brick you're about to lay or down the line the house could come tumbling down. You not only know what to do but how to do it. Great! So you've just built a very well-tuned automobile in your mind that will help you travel down the road to success. Now here's the fuel—the attitude that will guide you as you travel.

THE ATTITUDE

You must live immediately. You must live deliberately. Don't walk through life mindlessly driven by habit—this is as careless as driving without paying attention. Always know what you're doing, and you'll always know where you're going. If you spend a lot of time asking yourself, "Why did I say or do that?" then you're not paying attention. Your "habit head" is running the show.

Live deliberately, with immediacy, and make your actions and decisions count. In this way you can consciously pave the path you need to get where you want to go. Far too often we miss the exit to success because we're asleep at the wheel. Get off the hamster wheel of monotonous thinking, and blaze the path you intend for yourself. This is the only path that will get you where you want to go. Most importantly, you need to build the road yourself. Relying on someone else's standards and accepting them as your only option dooms you to a life of mediocrity. Pick your destination, build the road to get there step by step then drive with commitment and precision. The choice is yours.

Please Visit www.LifeTeamStrategy.com

This is where the power of living and thinking from your Hara comes into play. Don't live from your head or your heart—live from your Hara. Your head is the source of doubt and confusion, your heart, the house of impulsivity. But your Hara is the palace of confidence and balance, the foundation upon which your life is built. As your life is filled with those forces that increase your stability, your Hara becomes more balanced and strengthens. As it strengthens and your confidence builds, it becomes better able to support you on your journey toward your goals. Think of it: a foundation that actually becomes stronger as the building is constructed. The stronger the foundation, the higher the building can go. Live and breathe from your Hara, and ride the wave of confidence that comes out of the power of being balanced.

Now ask yourself again, "What do I want?" "What is my goal?" Name it. See it. Feel it. If it isn't real in your head, it sure as hell doesn't have a chance of being real in your life. We are more likely to believe in the things we can see and feel. This is why it is so important that our goals be as real in our minds as our own heartbeat is in our chest. But to truly live with as much power as possible, we need to be tumor free so no energy is taken away from creating what we really want.

THE "NO-YOU-CAN'T RANT"

You have the goal seared in your head now. But how bad do you want it? Are doubts still getting in your way? Are you subjecting yourself to the "No-you-can't rant," either from your own mind or the pessimism of others? This toxic waste dump of internal **Shouting** cheers for your failure with chants like, "You can't do that," "What do you want to do that for?" "Why don't you be more realistic?" or any other thought designed to kick your **Starter** in the crotch and rob you of your passion for success. Remember to ask yourself: Am I a victim or victor? You'd better know the answer by now. Victim thinking fuels the "No-you-can't rant." If you are writing the story of the victor, then leave these negative, defeatist passages out. No syrup in the gas tank on your road to success. So since you can't use them, lose them, then replace them.

"Can't" is the **Shouter**'s mantra, a powerless word that convinces you that something is out of your grasp. Take a minute and say aloud a list of things you think you can't do. For example, "I can't ski," "I can't do math well," "I can't lose weight," etc. After that minute is up, go back and repeat as many of the "I can'ts" that you remember. But this time replace the word "can't" with the word

Please Visit www.LifeTeamStrategy.com

"won't." Now your phrases sound like, "I won't ski," "I won't do math well" and "I won't lose weight." What's the difference between these two statements? One is **Shouting** and robs you of power, while the other is **Starting**, which takes responsibility and gives you that power back. You realize that you have simply chosen not to take the steps to do something. So "can't" no more. You clearly can do it if you choose to.

Now you're equipped to blow out the "No-you-can't rant" as easily as a hurricane blows out a candle. Your desire to reach your goal must exceed the strength of your doubts. Achieving your goal has to be the most important thing in your life. I know this sounds extreme, but only this level of commitment will guarantee that you won't give up. If you want to achieve your dreams more than you want to breathe, there is nothing that can stop you.

Living from your Hara means you're living from the place within you that is committed to sustaining your life. You live successfully by eating when hungry, sleeping when tired and breathing. With this thinking, achieving less than everything you're capable of is the same as suffocating. You are already used to breathing, now it's time to get used to succeeding. Learn **Starter** thinking, think success, talk success, breathe success, act success and live success. Before long it will become second nature.

Now you have your goal, but when it comes to goal attainment, your focus needs to be solely on the goal and its completion. Spending too much time bouncing between thoughts of either success or failure is like driving down the highway with the parking brake on. When your only consideration is success, you're driving with the pedal to the metal without the consideration of slowing down. When thoughts of doubt or failure enter, of course it will slow you down. Eventually when your thoughts linger on notions of failure long enough, you will run yourself off the road because you lost your focus.

THE CREDIBLE CAN'T

One of the most dangerous can'ts is "The Credible Can't." It occurs when we accept someone else's opinion that something CAN'T be done in one area simply because we value that person's opinion in another. Once a person has proven himself or herself to be a **Starter** and thus credible in our eyes, we often mistakenly grant them generalized credibility. This occurs when we assume that because a person demonstrates superior competence in one area, they must be excellent in other areas as well. This also occurs when you so admire a person in one area that

Please Visit www.LifeTeamStrategy.com

you begin to idealize them to the point that you want him or her to be everything to you.

In truth, none of us is perfect in all areas nor do we need to be. One of my heroes, Mahatma Gandhi, was a **Starter** for the nation of India but a **Shover** to his children whom he neglected while fighting for his country's independence. He saved his nation, but many of his children ended up resenting him. There are also plenty of professional sports figures that are **Starters** in terms of the sport they play but are **Sitters** or **Shouters** in their personal lives. I hope you realize now that when you give people credibility in areas where they haven't earned it, you're likely to end up getting and following bad advice.

When it comes to your own potential, any advice in the form of the phrase "You CAN'T do that because..." is bad advice, unless it comes from a police officer or a judge. Beyond those few exceptions, you typically get such advice from a person whose only basis for it is their own experience of having never done it.

First of all, allow the facts to speak for themselves, and only trust demonstrated credibility. "Trust me" is an insufficient reason to take someone's advice. Also be willing to allow others their imperfections and don't dismiss their credibility in one area simply because of their imperfections in others.

I have a different role model for each area of my life because one person doesn't have all the answers. It is when we follow one person blindly into all areas of life that we become disillusioned when we set such unreasonable expectations for another person. For example, in spite of the fact that former President Bill Clinton couldn't spell "monogamy" with a dictionary, he has superior leadership skills.

I'm not justifying anyone's behavior here. I'm simply highlighting the importance of being very clear that when you follow someone's lead, make sure they have the credibility to lead you in the area you want to follow them. The way you determine whether someone's advice to you is credible or not is to simply ask them what results they have experienced from following that same advice. If Donald Trump gave me advice about real estate, I'd probably take it because the results speak for themselves. If he told me the ten steps for making a marriage last, I would ask him flat out to give me examples on how those steps worked for him.

One sure fire way to determine that someone lacks credibility in a certain area is whenever the word CAN'T escapes their lips. History is filled with inventors who were told by the experts of their day that their pursuits were foolish. Had

Please Visit www.LifeTeamStrategy.com

they given credibility to those CAN'Ts, we might not have the luxury of the light bulb, the airplane, or the automobile.

Those who spend their lives saying something CAN'T be done end up eating the dust of those who eventually do it. Never give up on your dream because someone else is unable to see it in themselves or in you. Give credibility to your dreams not your doubts.

Your Big "But"

A strong runner-up to the "No-You-Can't Rant" is having a big "But." It has been my experience that a person's dreams are killed by excuses as much as any other reason. I've encountered people with incredible ability and so little to show for it. The magic ingredient to their lack of fulfillment is their tendency to **Shout** excuses that kill their desire and lead to a lack of action.

When I ask these **Shouters** what they're doing to make their dreams reality, they give me a list of excuses as to why they haven't begun, why they can't begin, or why it would never happen anyway. What it must be like to go through life like this, being one's own worst enemy.

Could you imagine a carpenter spending all his time thinking about why all the nails are going to pop up before even driving the first one, or an artist telling himself that all his paint is just going to run anyway so why bother. I've heard some parents justify not disciplining their children with the excuse, "Well they're just going to do it anyway."

When I talk of excuses I'm talking about the reasons we use to justify our own inaction. We all walk around with our "buts" in front of us, and they end up having more say in where we go than our dreams do. Some of the "buts" we throw in front of ourselves to prevent us from moving forward in life are, "But what about this?" or "But what about that?" These reasons that keep us stuck in life, when held up to the light, are as transparent as a politician's campaign promises. If you are your own worst enemy in this regard, it's time to wake up and smell the horse poop you're shoveling.

When I was in grade school I was surrounded by mostly negative people, which really infected my thinking. I can recall several adults telling me, "Brian, you are your own worst enemy." I was very pessimistic and had dismally low self-esteem. But I played a major part in it, too. Instead of challenging the input and looking to prove it wrong, I looked for reasons why it might be true and ended up reinforcing it. I find this tendency occurs in lots of people. If a child believes he's stupid, he often seeks out evidence to support it and acquires a host of excuses as to why it is necessary to stay that way.

As an adult I remember an interesting encounter that occurred while I was on my lunch break from my job at the time. I struck up a conversation with the young man who was working the buffet that day. He looked fresh out of high school and ripe for college. One of my questions to him was, "Are you still going to school?" He quickly replied, "Oh, I'm no good at school." "What do you mean?" I asked. "Well, I'm dyslexic," he replied. I asked him what that had to do with it. I quickly pointed out to him that there are dyslexics who run major corporations and accomplish many other great feats. He quickly followed up with another excuse, "Well, the teachers didn't like me anyway. They wouldn't help me." It occurred to me that if I pursued this further I would likely encounter more excuses. I quickly deduced that dyslexia wasn't this young man's problem—it was only his excuse.

Our lives are punctuated by our own excuses as well as the excuses of others. When we are children we hear excuses from our parents, such as "Because I said so" or "Because I'm the parent." These are excuses they use so they don't have to explain themselves. As we grow up we begin developing excuses of our own: "I don't feel good" or "I already have plans." As our lives change so do our excuses. When we develop relationships we must invent new excuses; when we don't have a good one we ask for advice from others. We're often met with an eagerness to help us out in our time of "excuslessness." When we get our first job we find excuses for getting out of work. When we want to get out of an uncomfortable situation, still more excuses. What's with all the excuses? Why are we always making excuses at the expense of relationships, honesty and, even worse, the quality of our lives?

Failure to take responsibility dooms us to continue the same pattern of behavior and thus experience the same unfortunate results. Excuses prevent **Sitters** from becoming **Starters** and **Shouters** from even getting started. I have a brother who blames everyone for his failures but insists on taking all the credit for his successes. Until he realizes the role he plays in his own results and the role others play in his successes, he will forever lack the wisdom of how to bring together the required resources to create and sustain the change he wants.

Is it a wonder why the U.S. Congress is a textbook study in stagnation? Congress is this country's premier blame factory. They are more interested in finger-pointing and fault-finding than problem-solving. Its members put more emphasis in being the sole author of the solution than of focusing on just being part of it. Even geese understand that you have to take turns being the leader—when they fly south for the winter in "V" formation, they take turns in the lead position. The two dominant political parties in this country act more like two warring countries than members of the same community. They spend more time fondling their own egos than tending to their constituents.

What power does a "but" have? This single word had the power to make the possible impossible. We can listen to 20 good reasons why something is possible. Then we respond with "but" and, in our own minds, blow all 20 out of the water.

"But" has the power to create failure and unhappiness by preventing you from going after the things you want. Why does a "but" have that much power? Because perception is reality. When we see anything through the lens of danger, then that's what we respond to and base our decisions on. If our choices are to be made based on the expectation of worst possible outcomes, then we'll never do anything.

However, "buts" are not entirely hopeless. It is possible to gain power from a "but"—it all depends on how you use it. "Buts" can actually be used to increase your options instead of always limiting them. For example, you can use phrases such as *"But what if things could turn out exactly as I wanted?"* The follow up question would be, *"Then how will I make it happen?"*

The next important step is instead of using a "but" to find exceptions, start looking for exceptions to the "but." Make the most complete list you can of the excuses you use. When you're satisfied with your list, take on each excuse one at a time. Let's say one of your excuses is "I don't want to ask another person out on a date because I'm afraid I'll be rejected." Your next step is to list as many exceptions to that excuse as possible. In the past you may have used an excuse to disprove the rule, now you're doing exactly the opposite—you're actively using the rule to disprove the excuse. A little self-imposed reverse psychology if you will.

After you've identified enough exceptions to the excuse, it is time to write out what it will take to create the new exception. Before you know it you are caught up in the process of planning and achieving a goal instead of building up an excuse. This is a wonderful "but" buster and can really benefit you, but only if you want it to.

WHERE TO GO FROM "NO"

After successfully navigating the "can'ts" and "buts" of your life, you must then learn how to effectively use one of the most powerful words on Earth, the word

Please Visit www.LifeTeamStrategy.com

"no." Do you ever have difficulty saying "no" to others? How about when someone says "no" to you? Some people treat the word "no" like kryptonite and let it suck the energy out of them whenever they hear it. Others use it as an incentive to keep going. In other words, you can hear "no" as **Shouting** or **Starting**. Starters hear "no" as **an** answer not **the** answer. A person who says "no" to you is telling you more about themselves than they are about you. What they're saying is that their personal criteria doesn't allow them to give you what you want.

For example, I was working with a client who needed a job but wouldn't set up any job interviews because he was afraid of rejection. After questioning him about his fear, I discovered that he went into each interview with an all or nothing mindset. He would tell himself that this was the job he had to have and was therefore putting all his eggs in one basket and eliminating all other options for himself. What do you think this mindset did for him? It increased his stress level significantly because he treated every interview like his last chance. Since he told himself he had to have that particular job, when an employer didn't hire him he treated it like the interviewer punched him in the face.

Afterward he would **Shout** at himself by asking questions like "Why wasn't I good enough?" or "What was wrong with me?" Clearly I recommended that he refine his questions. If you think you aren't good enough, you begin to think you're not worthy of the job, which is clearly not the case.

He and I soon established that he still wanted a job in the field he was interviewing in, but since he wasn't being snatched up by employers it might have been because they were looking for something he currently wasn't providing. This by no means meant he couldn't provide it—just that he currently didn't. In this context I encouraged to him to interpret the word "no" as actually meaning "not yet."

Employers hire people whose qualifications are in line with what the position requires. If you don't have those qualifications, get them. The way to find out the qualifications you need to have is by asking what they are. I encouraged my client to call the individual he'd interviewed with, and instead of asking a self-deprecating question like "What was wrong with me?" ask the question "What would you have liked to see in my qualifications to make me desirable for your company?" The difference here is you're asking about your qualifications not about yourself. Qualifications are always something you can get more of. I have yet to meet the company interviewer who won't answer this question. They want people to know what they're looking for, otherwise they won't find the people they need. If you don't know where to get the experience or knowledge they recommend, then ask them where to get it.

Please Visit www.LifeTeamStrategy.com

This client's dilemma resulted from his interpretation of the word "no" as a judgment of his worth, which is the **Shouter** perspective. The truth as well as the **Starter** point of view is that people say "no" for themselves; they don't say it against you. A "no" is a boundary setter that tells you what a person is not willing to give. It is a reflection as much of their limits as it is of yours.

In fact, whenever I ask for help from someone who I thought was a **Starter** and they end up telling me "no," I often come right out to them and say, "Oh, I'm sorry. I thought you were someone else. I thought you were the person who was going to tell me 'yes.' I'll just keep looking then."

WHICH ONE ARE YOU?

Once you've gotten your "can'ts" and "buts" out of the way, there's still "one" other thing to consider. One of the most fascinating things you can pick up in conversation with people are the words they use to classify themselves, especially in terms of the one they believe themselves to be. If you listen to them closely, you can tell pretty quickly if the one they choose to be can help them become the one they're capable of being.

For instance, how many times have you heard someone say, "I'm not one of those people" or "Oh you're one of those." You may also have heard people identify themselves by saying "I'm the smart one" or referring to another by saying that "He or she is the cute one." I was raised in a large family and was repeatedly asked the same question by people outside the family: "Which one are you?" This question, believe it or not, has a much more profound meaning than "What's your name?" This question goes to the heart of not only who you are but also who you've been encouraged to be by the "Life Team" members you've chosen.

I decided to make a short list of the ones I've been introduced to over the years. It would be a good idea for you to take a mental inventory of how often you've heard them from others and who you've heard them from. Most importantly, you'll want to note which ones you've used to describe yourself.

So "Which one are you?" Are you, or have you ever met the:

Athletic one

Best one

Brightest one

Please Visit www.LifeTeamStrategy.com

Creative one

Crazy one

Dependable one

Dumb one

Fat one

First one

Funny one

Great one

Happy one

Independent one

Jealous one

Last one

Loud one

Middle one

Next one

New one

Normal one

Number one

One everybody turns to

One nobody talks about

Old one

Other one

Pretty one

Respectable one

Responsible one

Quiet one

Reliable one

Right one

Skinny one

Short one

Smart one

Sweet one

Successful one

Shy one

Talented one

Tall one

Thin one

This one

That one

Weird one

Wrong one

Young one

Or are you simply

THE ONE AND ONLY?

I began a tradition a few years ago when my second son, Aidan, was born. My first born, Zach, was afraid he'd lose my love to his brother and flat out asked me if he was still my favorite. I explained to him that he would always be my number one Zach, and his brother would be my number one Aidan. That way each of my children would always know that the answer to the question "Which one are you?" will always be "I am the number one me."

Whichever one you determine yourself to be, you must remember one thing: Who you are or who you've come to think of yourself as is a mere shadow of who you can become. The one you are now is not the one you will be forever. Who you are now is simply the seed for the one you are meant to be. If you're going to be one, be one who learns, grows, and helps everyone become better ones. If anyone can do it, you're the one.

At any moment in our lives our self-perception is informed by at least three things: who we were, who we are and who we can become. Although we live in the moment and are in closest proximity to who we are, we are by no means standing still. We not only are, we are also becoming. We are never without the opportunity to become whatever it is we strive to be. Of course, we are not perfect the way we are; if we were then we would have nothing to work toward. Every success, great or small, is built on each step we take toward it. Knowing who and where you are is an important first step. So who are you? What do you stand for? What is your life for?

I can give you some guidelines to help you begin to answer these questions. You can take these or leave them, but at least consider them. It is my belief that who you are is "now." Yes, *you* are now. You are the result of your experiences with life to this point and at this moment. You are adapting to the environment around you, including this book, and changing as a result. You are in a perpetual state of adaptation, so whatever now is, so you are as well.

What do you stand for? What battles do you fight? Do you fight to maintain your ego, for justice, for what? What will winning these battles get you? I know a few people who have succumb to the hard times in their lives and are so immersed in the black hole of victimhood that they fight to maintain this status. It becomes the meaning of their life, and their goal is to make others feel sorry for them. They are always complaining, feeling sorry for themselves and becoming outraged when others don't join them. They always argue when someone else's victimization takes center stage and the spotlight is removed from them. What will winning this battle get for them? It will get them a life of victimization, that's what. By failing to take control where they have it and not finding power through adversity, they are unable to achieve victory.

Please Visit www.LifeTeamStrategy.com

WHAT IS YOUR LIFE FOR?

What is your life for? I feel you can determine this by determining where your passion and ability meet. Every person is born enabled by his or her unique composite of biological magnificence with the ability to do at least one thing extremely well. However, this one thing usually only becomes apparent when the demands of our environment provides for its unveiling. As we've found, an upbringing that is filled with "can't programming" leaves us ill-equipped to explore our potential.

However, on some level I believe that every living thing is compelled in some way to do what it is designed to do best. Plants are compelled by design to produce oxygen and some a beautiful fragrance as well. Animals are compelled by their instincts to do what they're best at in order to play their unique part in the circle of life. As human beings I believe our passion and the ability to realize that passion compel us to do what we are each designed for.

What is passion? It is the focused drive that gets a person out of a burning house. The sheer determination that compels an athlete to ignore pain until a goal is achieved. Passion is the desire for something that is so strong you feel like you couldn't live without it. For some it is writing, painting, acting, playing a sport, etc. The one thing that gives their life more meaning than anything else that they can't live without is their passion. For me it is being of service to others in order to help them discover and maximize their own greatness. If I am not being of service to others, I might as well not be living. What is it that you are as compelled to do, as you are to continue breathing, but also have the ability to do? For me it's writing and public speaking. I thrive on communicating in any way possible. I give to others, and they give to me. I not only enjoy it—I also do this quite well. My passion and ability meet.

Some people struggle to define the purpose of their lives. I've learned firsthand that there is nothing that gets you out of bed in the morning faster and with greater vitality than a sense of purpose for your day and for your life. I walk through my day everyday with focus, clarity and an added bounce in my step while I watch others walk around tired, aimless and depressed. The only difference between me and them is that I know precisely what I'm doing it all for. So, what is the point of it all? Why bother getting up in the morning? There is only one answer to all of these questions, and the answer is "Whatever you want."

Think of a large sailing vessel on the ocean whose sense of direction depends on one simple little thing—a compass. All you need in order to give your life that

Please Visit www.LifeTeamStrategy.com

same sense of focus, direction and clarity of purpose is a master guiding principle for your life called a "Personal Mission Statement," or PMS for short.

Your PMS is a statement of the principle value in your life. My life was transformed when I developed my mission statement. I have told only a few people what my PMS is, and in order to help you begin to develop your own, I'm going to tell you as well. My Personal Mission Statement is "To Do Whatever It Takes to Relieve the Suffering of Others." Everything I do in life, which includes this book, is aimed toward supporting my PMS.

Now that you know what my PMS is, allow me to explain exactly how to construct one of your own. First and foremost a PMS is an action statement. It states the kind of action you will take in order to produce a specific result. In my case the action I'll take is "To Do Whatever It Takes," which means I will not stop until I find a solution. The result my action will produce is "to Relieve the Suffering of Others." Once you have a PMS, you aren't stuck with it. You can change it and refine it as you grow and your values change. What matters most is that your life is not simply supported by values, but by values you can apply.

With a powerful PMS you will find yourself becoming more focused and more effective because your entire mindset becomes one committed to action in order to obtain a measurable result. You're on a mission right now—to determine what your mission is, how you're going to carry it out and then doing it. Back it up with a Hara decision to see it through, and your life as well as the lives you touch will become better as a result.

THE THREE ATTITUDES FOR ACHIEVEMENT

You may have the ability and the passion, but do you have the stamina to go the distance? Whenever you plan for a trip, the issue is not whether you can complete the trip or not, the question is how are you going to do it? Once you've decided on a goal, there are three attitudes you can use to work toward accomplishing it. You can "Try," "Do your best" or you can "Do whatever it takes." Two of these attitudes are cancerous and deadly to your passion. One of these attitudes is the cure for the other two.

I'll tell you right now that if you "Try" to succeed, you will fail. By definition the word "try" means "attempt" not "completion." **Sitters** "try," **Starters** finish what they start. Accomplishing a goal is about completion and nothing less. You can recognize the "try" attitude by statements to yourself like, "I'll give it a shot" or "Well, at least I tried." If this is your attitude then don't bother. You will always proceed with hesitation and doubt if you "try."

A "Do your best" attitude is also insufficient because it implies that you have limits and that your best may not be enough. You are motivated by "I'll give it all I've got," when you may not know you actually have more to give. "I hope I have it in me," reveals that you doubt as to whether you do. These attitudes contain doubt—doubt creates hesitation, decreases motivation and leads to disaster. Even if you're focused on doing your best, you're still thinking in terms of limits. Your best only allows you to accomplish the goals you currently have the skills for. If you run a marathon when you're out of shape and don't perform well, you may conclude that your best was insufficient. However, some training can raise your level of ability and suddenly your best has been kicked up a notch. Your best is always relative to your preparedness to address the task at hand. It is not a hard and fast constant by which you can measure what you are ultimately capable of.

The "Do your best" and "try" attitudes leave you with easy excuses for falling short of your goal: "Well, at least I tried" or "As long as you did your best." Is this really what you're willing to settle for? Any attitude that doesn't propel you toward success is essentially programming you to quit before you've even started. By embracing this kind of thinking, you are enabling the **Sitter** in you, and you and I know that you are capable of so much more. One major difference between those who quit and those who succeed is that quitters always follow their own advice. They expect not to do well, and when they don't they say, "I should've trusted my instincts. I told you I couldn't do it." Well, guess what? All you proved was that failure thinking leads to failure, not that you couldn't do it. People who succeed always look toward what's possible and seek out whatever and whoever can provide the guidance toward their goal. **Starters** seek other **Starters**.

These "try" and "Do your best" attitudes allow us on some level to talk ourselves out of succeeding because they focus on our deficiencies. But deficits have nothing to do with our successes in life; it's our strengths that create our success. Our assumptions about our own limitations must never stand in the way of making a meaningful decision that can better our lives. Any limitation should be revealed through trial and learning—not self-doubt. We must tell ourselves, "I can and will do it because…" This is the only consideration when setting goals. Our primary strength, which is the key to any success, is the strength of our own determination to succeed. The stronger it is, the further our minds get from the option of quitting.

The attitude that will allow you to accomplish the goals you set for yourself is the "Do whatever it takes" attitude. You are guided by questions like "What do I have to do to get it done." You have taken the first and most important step toward reaching your goal. By making a Hara decision to succeed, you equip yourself with a commitment that is clear, strong and unbreakable. Your commitment must be strong enough to support you. Resolving to do whatever it takes leaves no room for doubt because with it you are focused on taking the necessary steps and acquiring the skills that will ensure success. Any goal is attainable if the tasks required for its completion are accomplished. Your best may not include all of the necessary skills now. But the "Do whatever it takes" mentality commits you to acquiring them in the process of attaining your goal. This is the most powerful cognitive chemo cure I know of.

Another profound benefit of this attitude is that its sole focus is on achieving the goal and not on yourself. You no longer think me, me, me; instead, you think success, success, success. That way the "No-you-can't rant" doesn't have a chance because the process of goal completion is no longer about you. You may think that the purpose of achieving the goal is to satisfy some personal desire. Be that as it may, you can't derive satisfaction from attaining a goal that hasn't been reached yet, so leave your satisfaction aside and concentrate on what it will take to get there. If you focus on yourself, you take your eye off the goal. If you are thinking of yourself, make sure it is only to make sure you are doing whatever it takes to succeed.

Of course, this attitude will take work to embody and master. It isn't made any easier if you have a low tolerance for frustration. The uncontrollables of life will challenge you, including the simple things like red lights and the more complicated like poor attitudes of people in charge or a change in your health. But the important thing to remember is that these things are only obstacles. Your progress will not always be smooth, and it may plateau from time to time, but always stay on the path toward your goal. If there is one thing I learned from the experience of cancer it's that no matter how treacherous the road ahead appears, your circumstances are never bigger than you are. If an acorn can grow to become an enormous oak tree, you can reach any goal you set for yourself no matter how big it is. Like the acorn, all you require to become everything you're capable of are the right circumstances for growth and the patience to sustain the journey. Once you establish those, it's only a matter of time.

Remember there are no impossibilities, only varying degrees of difficulty. If you are committed to doing whatever it takes, the road will become less difficult as your commitment increases. Just remember that the moment you make a Hara decision, there is no turning back. There is only one way out: success. You must succeed, you're going to succeed, you've chosen to succeed.

Please Visit www.LifeTeamStrategy.com

The Failure Fallacy

Here are a few thoughts to help solidify your "Do whatever it takes" attitude. The common denominator in the short lifespan of the commitment level of the "Try" and "Do your best" attitudes is the role that the fear of failure plays.

I'm going to let you in on a little know fact: Failure doesn't exist, but quitting does. The only time your goals are not achieved is when you give up the pursuit. Legendary football coach Vince Lombardi was once quoted as saying, "We didn't lose the game, we just ran out of time." Neither he nor his team ever gave up. In spite of what some others may think, they're pursuit of excellence wasn't measured by the outcome of one game because the goal was still in sight and the journey continued.

Think about it: You only fail if you lose something. Your efforts may not pay off immediately, but when your effort doesn't produce, you haven't lost anything. You're simply right back where you started. No win, no lose, you're even.

When asked how he dealt with the repeated failure in his efforts to invent the lightbulb, Thomas Edison said, "I never failed. I just found 10,000 ways to do it wrong." He understood that mistakes are like carving a statue: Get rid of the stuff that won't help the final product, and what you're left with is exactly what you want.

The results of any effort are still results whether they were the ones you wanted or not. Their value lies in the fact that they reveal what worked and what didn't. Continue doing what worked and change what didn't and you are that much closer to achieving the results you desire. It may take 10,000 times, but if you persevere you will succeed.

Look at it as though you are an Olympic hurdler. There are plenty of hurdles placed in your way as you pursue the finish line. Every single hurdle is part of the race, and each one, when approached in the right way, can be overcome. Lombardi and Edison approached their hurdles in the right way; as a result, they reached the finish line.

Finding the Passion Within You: Coming up for Air

What is unfortunate is that some people can't muster up the level of commitment that keeps their energy high while pursuing their goal. Therefore, I developed an

Please Visit www.LifeTeamStrategy.com

exercise that can show you just how to think and feel with passion and also to train your mind to experience what absolute single-pointed focus feels like. I call it "Coming up for air." But before I teach you the exercise, I want to tell you the event in my life that inspired this exercise.

One evening about seven years ago, my wife and I were invited to my sister's house for dinner because my father had come down to visit. My now ex-brother-in-law was a wonderful cook, and I used to partake of his hospitality anytime I had the opportunity. Well, one of his best side dishes was a rice concoction mixed with a whole lot of butter, which made it very thick. As it turned out, I was eating the rice a little too fast, and when I swallowed it, it was so thick that it formed a ball in my throat and lodged there. I immediately began choking, but I couldn't make a sound. I took a drink, but the soda just filled my mouth because it couldn't dislodge the rice. I was trying not to make a scene because I didn't want to believe what was happening. My relatives were talking and laughing and had no idea what was going on. When I realized I was in trouble, I began pounding my throat with one hand and motioning for help with the other.

This is the ironic part: I was sitting next to my wife, who is a registered nurse and works at a hospital, and my father, who is a former deputy fire chief and emergency medical technician. When I motioned for help, neither of them moved—it was my sister on the other end of the table who acted. She got up and ran around behind my chair. She stood me up and gave a quick thrust to my abdomen. Let's just say her tablecloth was never the same again. After I caught my breath, I asked my wife and father why they just sat there? My wife said she was shocked, and my dad said he thought I was kidding.

Either way, who did what wasn't as important as what I learned from that experience. Later that night I reflected upon what had happened and what was going through my mind as I was struggling for air. As I was sitting there fighting to breathe, I realized that I was unable to think of anything else. I was completely focused on one thing and one thing only: getting that breath. My body tensed up as my adrenaline shot up, and I became focused on that one goal. If you're familiar with the saying, "Some of the best lessons are learned the hard way," this clearly qualifies as one of them. The ability for single-minded purpose was driven into me more than ever by this incident. I began thinking about how I might be able to demonstrate and teach this level of focus and determination in pursuit of a single goal. It was difficult. I clearly couldn't invite people to choke themselves to fully appreciate this experience. But I was able to come up with something that is very close, and I'd like you to do it now.

Please Visit www.LifeTeamStrategy.com

If you have asthma, don't do this; there is an alternative I will explain to you afterward. For everyone else, have someone read the directions to you as you complete the exercise so you'll be surprised.

Take in a deep, cleansing breath to help yourself relax, and let it out. Now as quickly as possible, I want you to take in the deepest breath you possibly can, then quickly blow it all out and, when it's all out, hold it out. Don't take a breath in no matter how badly you want to. Pay attention as the following chain of events begin to take place. You will begin to feel extreme tension in your chest and throat that begins to build and increase. Soon every inch of your body will start focusing on achieving one goal and compelling you to act to act on it. The moment you know what you want to do more than anything else, go ahead and do it. (I'm assuming you've chosen to take a breath.)

Now think about what was happening in your body and your mind. If you're like everyone else who's done the exercise, the only thought in your mind was your desire to take a breath. Your thoughts were focused on one thing, and there was a sense of urgency. You have to get that breath, and you have to act now to get it.

During the time you couldn't breathe, you probably had an increased sense of focus and mental commitment that was virtually unbreakable. Imagine how powerful your determination would be if you apply this feeling to the pursuit of your goal. It would be nearly impossible to stop you. If you can recall the sense of urgency and focus that you just experienced as you thought about your desire to get that breath, I want you to do so. Now with that same focus, sense of urgency and commitment, replace the desire for that breath with a desire for achieving your goal. Even better, do the exercise again, and when you start thinking about how bad you want to breathe, replace your desire for a breath with the desire for your goal. What you will be experiencing is focused, single minded, unbridled passion for whatever your mind is set on. When you proceed with this kind of energy toward your goals, what in the world can stop you?

For those of you with asthma, I recommend that the next time you have to go to the bathroom, you should hold it as long as possible. Soon you will experience the same sense of urgency and single-minded focus as is produced in the previous example.

THE DOUBLE H LIST

I hope that at this point you are well on the road to becoming unscrewed and ridding your mind of the **Shoving** and **Shouting** that holds you back. Now I offer you yet another exercise that will help you cure nearly any cancerous influence in your psychological and emotional life.

I discovered early in my recovery the importance of identifying the negative, often toxic influences in my life as well as specifically identifying the harm they do. Some of these toxic influences are subtle, while others are more obvious. I created an exercise to help identify the effects of both the subtle and the obvious attacks on your self-esteem. Actually, the creation of this exercise was spontaneous, an on-the-spot solution to a friend's problem.

I was speaking to this friend when she brought up the issue of the relationship she was currently involved in with her father. Her father had been an alcoholic her entire life and, as such, had provided mostly toxicity to her development as a person. Now in her adult life, her attempts to establish boundaries between him and herself had been difficult as he preys upon her sense of family loyalty to keep her from distancing herself from him. He's been nothing but a **Shover** and a **Shouter** her entire life.

Her self-concept and self-esteem are continuously shaken whenever they speak. Her efforts to assert herself and achieve resolution with him for past hurts in order for their relationship to heal and grow have been met only with defensiveness and vicious verbal attacks on his part. The point had finally been reached where she felt it was time to begin distancing herself from him, but she was unsure how to do it.

After further discussion on the issue, my friend realized why she was having such difficulty distancing herself from him. She was so used to her father's presence in her life that, in spite of the fact she wanted less of it, she was having difficulty imagining her life without it and precisely what changes could take place that would be a significant improvement over the way things currently were.

I came up with an exercise for her to do that would help her sort out precisely what she was having difficulty picturing. I call this exercise the "Double H List." I will explain it to you from the standpoint of how I instructed my friend to use it.

I instructed her to get a piece of paper and title it "Having Dad in My Life" (you can title it according to whatever challenge you are currently facing). I then told her to make two columns to represent her two H's. The first column is titled "Help," the second one, "Hurt." I then assigned her a task. She was to find a quiet place where she wouldn't be interrupted so her mind could work without distraction. I urged her not to approach this analytically as this was sure to slow the process.

Once she was ready, she was to begin with the first column and ask herself, "How is having my dad in my life helpful to me?" She was then told to brainstorm—write whatever came to her mind without analyzing any one item and not stopping until she absolutely ran out of things. Afterward she was to take a few minutes to just sit and breathe, giving her mind time to settle and finish that part of the activity.

Next she would move to column two and ask, "How is having my dad in my life hurtful to me?" She then proceeded as she did with column one. By no means should you confine your list to one sheet of paper. You may be surprised by how things get uncovered when you get the surface thoughts out of the way. You may end up with several pages if you really let your mind work, so be prepared with several sheets so you don't have to stop to get more.

When she was done with the second column and had taken a few minutes to let the listing portion of the exercise be completed, it was time to look back at what she had written. First she needed to look at which list is longer. This was the first hint as to the value this relationship holds in her life. Next she was to look at each column and each item. When looking at the items in the "HELP" column, she asked these questions about each item:

1. **What does this benefit add to my life?**
2. **Is this a benefit I can do without?**
3. **How will my life be different without it?**
4. **Can I get this benefit from someone or something else?**

When answering the questions about the items in the "HURT" column, she asked these questions:

1. **What is it costing me to allow this influence in my life?**
2. **How will my life be improved by eliminating or reducing my exposure to it?**
3. **What steps must I take to eliminate or reduce it in my life?**
4. **How will this benefit my self-esteem?**

Please Visit www.LifeTeamStrategy.com

This exercise proved to be very useful in helping her externalize the issue with her father. By putting each list in writing, she was able to objectively weigh the benefits of limiting contact with her father because her opposing thoughts of loyalty to her father no longer had to compete for the same space in her mind.

If you were to create a "Double H List" for any issue you where struggling with, from deciding the benefits of a relationship in your life to deciding whether or not to pursue a certain goal, what would it be about? This one exercise can be very effective at allowing you to see the whole picture and make a more complete and informed decision about what to do to resolve the issue.

Too often simply by keeping the facts locked up in your head, you make it more difficult to objectively sort something out. Think of it as a group of people all trying to get comfortable in a telephone booth—there is a lot of discomfort, aggravation and elbowing. Only after one person steps out of the booth is it easier for him or her to view the problem and give it proper perspective.

This is the same as taking the issue out of your head where it's competing for airtime with other concerns and putting it on paper so you can give it your undivided attention. This helped my friend achieve the perspective she needed and begin to prioritize the steps she needed to take to minimize the negative impact her father was having on her self-esteem.

Here is another way you can use the "Double H List," which is more in line with what we've been discussing. Prepare your list as you did before with your "Help" and "Hurt" columns. Title your list with a goal you're currently having trouble accomplishing. In the "Help" column, list the thoughts, decisions and actions that are helping your progress toward achieving your goal. Under the "Hurt" column, list all of your thoughts, decisions and actions that are working against you. This will help you determine quickly if you're doing more **Starting** or **Shouting**. This doesn't have to be completed in a single sitting because you might not be fully aware of some of the things you're saying or doing until you catch yourself doing them. Or you may not be willing to admit you're doing them. Fold up your list, and keep it with you so you'll have it when these thoughts and behaviors take place. If you really want to make things interesting, make a list of the people on your Life Team that "Help" you in your pursuit of the goal and those that "Hurt" you.

Whenever you hear yourself saying things like, "Why do I bother" or anything self-defeating, write it down immediately. By doing so, your "Double H List" becomes your tool for becoming more aware of your self-defeating behavior so you can hold yourself accountable for it. If you can't identify it, you can't stop doing it. By holding yourself accountable for the helpful things as well as the

Please Visit www.LifeTeamStrategy.com

hurtful things, you can concentrate on doing the helpful things more and the hurtful things less. This is a sure-fire way of cleaning out your toolbox so only the sharpest tools remain.

As your "Help" list gets longer and your "Hurt" list gets shorter, you will reach your goal faster. By working on your list daily you gradually increase your self-awareness and effectiveness until you become a success machine. In a perfect world we would only engage in those beliefs and behaviors that help us. Unfortunately the human mind is full of hiccups. However, by utilizing the "Double H List," you can have a lot fewer hiccups than most people.

7

Meaning Mastery

I've found that one of the best ways to shape our present as well as our future is by looking to those people who have already done that which we're intending to do in order to gather a bit of their wisdom. In this case, let's look to the late psychotherapist Virginia Satir who once said, "There is no such thing as a meaningful experience, we create meaning."

Think about the profound importance of that statement. Now in order to play with your mind a little more I'm going to ask you a question. And the answer to this question is one of the keys to unleashing everything you will ever need to know to become the **Starter** you are meant to be and create a life that is overflowing with the very stuff that makes life worth living.

Understanding the answer to this question is the foundation for everything that is to follow. If you don't get the answer right away there is no need to commit Hara-kiri over it. If you don't know what Hara-kiri is, chances are you don't want to know. Anyway, are you ready for the question? Here it is...

Imagine you are watching a tree, a tree with branches that are slowly bending back and forth as the wind gently blows through them. Now the question I have to ask of you is simply this: What is moving? Is the tree moving, or is the wind moving? Take a few seconds before you answer to fully understand the question. Do you have an answer? Well, which is moving, the wind or the tree? The answer is, your mind is moving. Did you get that? It is your mind that is moving, not the tree or the wind.

Think of your mind as an experience processor. Through the senses of sight, smell, sound, taste and touch, the information you take in is synergistically combined in your mind. Your mind then takes all of this information and adds the magic ingredient that is the final stroke of the paintbrush of experience. Your mind adds meaning.

You perceive movement in a tree, the wind or anything else because you've learned that certain sensory information is referred to as something called movement. Do you follow me? If you're not sure, stick with me; you'll understand more as we go along. If you do understand it, great—you're well on your way.

All you really need to understand at this point is that:

The sum of all your fears
Lies squarely between your ears.

And the key to unlocking the door to your dreams
Is in realizing that not all is as it seems.

And the secret to changing the way things seem
Is by changing the way you think things mean.

All right, so the last phrase isn't grammatically correct, but you get the point. So what are we talking about here? We're talking about the stuff that makes life worth living. And that stuff is called meaning. I'll show you how to extract the greatest quality of life from each and every day that you spend on this beautiful orb we call Earth simply by mastering the way you decide what life is going to mean to you. At this point I recommend that you ask yourself a few important questions:

1. What is the key aspect of a happy life?

2. How can I maximize my energy and avoid burnout?

3. How can I become better and better every single day?

Keep those questions in your mind because we're going to discover some answers to them as we proceed.

THE TRUTH SHALL SET YOU FREE! OR WILL IT?

Now I'd like to get your opinion on something. I'd like to know what meaning, if any, the following statement has for you: "The truth shall set you free." Do you agree with that statement? Why? Why not? It's a statement you may have heard many times before but never taken the time to examine. So let's think a little more about it.

Please Visit www.LifeTeamStrategy.com

What if the truth is that you've been diagnosed with terminal cancer and you have six months to live? Where is the freedom in that truth? What if the truth is that you've just been fired from a job you've given your heart and soul to for the past 20 years? Where is the freedom to be found there? The fact of the matter is that the truth has nothing to do with your freedom in either case. What sets you free is the meaning you assign to that truth. It is the meaning that sets you free.

The meaning you choose can create obstacles or opportunities, hindrance or hope. It can make you bitter or it can make you better. It's your choice. I've met people who've been given a terminal diagnosis and spent the last days of their lives bitter and resentful. I've also met people who spent the time making sure that those days were filled with every last drop of joy that could be squeezed out of them.

The only difference between these people is the meaning they assigned to the truth that was given to them and, therefore, the opportunities they believed were available to them. In the example of losing a job after 20 years, all you have to do is watch the evening news to see how some people react to that truth. Some people return to their previous place of employment with a loaded gun and tragically use their coworkers for target practice.

Others spend a few days reflecting on what's happened and then decide to start their own business, go back to school or find an entirely different job altogether. One reaction is fueled by blame and rage, the other by contemplation, searching for options and seeking resolution. The key, again, is meaning.

THE MEANING OF LIFE

Since the dawn of human thought people have pondered a single question, "What is the meaning of life?" Well, what is it? Do you have an answer? My answer is simple—the meaning of life is whatever it means to you. And your meaning can change daily, thus changing the direction as well as the quality of your experience and your life.

If you believe that life's a bitch and then you die then that's exactly the kind of life you'll have. You can believe that life doesn't give you more than you can handle or you can believe that life purposely gives you more than you can handle to enable you to grow into the person that can handle it. The key to a meaningful life lies in what we do with the experience of the resistance we face.

After all, our lives are a series of experiences, but those experiences teach us nothing unless we assign some sort of meaning to them. How do you think you

Please Visit www.LifeTeamStrategy.com

would define the word "meaning" if someone asked you to do so? Every time I've asked someone to define "meaning," they've typically explained it as the meaning or understanding of words in a conversation. But when I pressed them to define meaning as it applies to life specifically, they weren't sure where to go.

The point being that it's difficult to master anything, especially meaning, when you don't even know what it is. So, for the purpose of this discussion and to keep you and I on the same page, let's define meaning as "the value you assign to your experiences." Experiences of good or bad, right or wrong are all judgments about the value of those experiences, and the value you place on an experience determines the meaning it has for you.

I've listened to discussions between movie critics who argue their point about a movie as though they were arguing to save their own lives. Other people listening might say it's just a stupid movie. Who's right? I imagine it depends upon what the movie meant to you. We assign meaning to everything, and we actively seek out experiences that have meaning for us. Meaning is the most powerful motivator there is.

Napoleon Bonaparte once said, "I was amazed the day I discovered that men will die for ribbons." What were the men he spoke of actually dying for? Were they dying for a piece of fabric with a little piece of metal dangling from it? No—they were dying in the pursuit of the honor, pride or whatever other meaning they assigned to earning the medal.

For some people a life without meaning is not worth living, for others a life with meaning can be worth losing in defense of that meaning. Take some time to think about that. What are some of the things you've done because of what it meant to you to do it? What causes do you support or participate in because of how much it means to you? What do you do for a living, how do you make your money? Why do you do that? Why not something else? Think about it.

THE EDGE

Have you thought about it? Based on your answers, is meaning positive or negative? Actually it's both. It all depends on the meaning you create. What determines the experience you have resides solely between your ears. Let's do a visualization exercise that will allow you to experience the actual creation of meaning in your own mind. Are you ready?

This exercise requires you to be standing up with your eyes closed, so it's advisable to have someone slowly read this exercise to you so you can get the full experience of it. Start by closing your eyes. Take in a deep cleansing breath...and let it out. Just relax. Now I want you to begin to construct a very quiet comforting place in your mind. Where are you standing? Are you standing on grass, sand or dirt? Are you wearing shoes, or are your bare feet gently pressing against the ground?

Is it daytime or nighttime? What's the weather like? Is it warm, or is there a slight chill in the air? What sounds do you hear? Do you hear the sounds of birds singing, children laughing? The sound of the wind blowing through a nearby tree? Take a moment to just enjoy the scene you've created for yourself. All the while taking nice, long, deep breaths and taking the time to picture the image clearly in your mind before continuing.

Now I want you to imagine that you hear the sound of the ocean not too far off in the distance. You can hear the distinct crashing sound of the waves hitting the shore. I want you to imagine walking toward the sound of the ocean. After walking a short way in your mind, I want you to stop. Now imagine that you've just stopped in the nick of time because your toes are resting on the edge of a 100-foot cliff. Imagine that you look down slightly and see all of the sharp rocks at the bottom.

How are you feeling inside with this sudden realization? Do you want to back away slowly? What do you want to do? Again, in your mind only, gently take one step backward, then another, until you're comfortably away from the edge of the cliff.

Now take another deep breath in...then blow it out and relax. Start to realize that you're not at the edge of a cliff. Nor are you standing on a beach, in a field or wherever it is you put yourself. You are safe and sound, on solid ground in a very familiar place. Now slowly open your eyes.

What happened to you during this exercise? How did you react? Did the level of tension in your body change? Did your heart begin to beat faster at any point? If it did, at what point? No matter what reactions you experienced, ask yourself the following questions: "Why did I react that way?" "What was I reacting to?" "Were the images in my mind imaginary or real?" "Where was I really?"

Was your experience of this exercise imaginary or real? The answer is it doesn't make a difference. Your mind and body can't tell the difference between an imaginary experience and a real one. Why else do you think we get terrified by nightmares while lying in the comfort of our own beds? It's because we don't respond to reality—we respond to our perception of reality. So what does this mean for your life? It means that you are the architect of your everyday life.

What you were responding to was the meaning you assigned to the images you created in your mind. Certain images may have meant peace and serenity, while

Please Visit www.LifeTeamStrategy.com

other images meant danger. It all depends on the context. An ordinary person standing on a cliff may be overcome with panic, while a different person who happens to be carrying a hang glider may be energized with excitement because a cliff is exactly what he or she is looking for. The ultimate lesson to take away from this exercise is that the meaning you create determines the experience you have.

It stands to reason that emotions aren't things that happen to you but things that you do. So in actuality you don't get frightened, you practice frightening. There are certain thoughts you need to be thinking, certain images you need to be seeing in order to frighten yourself. Think of all the thoughts that go through your mind as you're walking alone at night.

You choose to be angry or happy just as you choose to engage in joy and self-respect. You choose your life based on what you choose to pay attention to and, most important, the meaning you choose to assign to it. The lesson here is simply this: If you become a master of your own meaning, you will become a master of your life.

Angel Training

I created a concept that allowed me to truly see the hardship in my life as happening for me instead of to me. This concept has also been very useful to others I've worked with that were going through some pretty rough periods in their lives, either because of a divorce, the death of a loved one, a life-threatening illness, a bankruptcy or numerous other life crises.

The questions I've been asked most often by these individuals time and time again are: "Why is this happening to me?" and "Why is God doing this to me?" I've thought long and hard on appropriate answers to those questions. Clearly those questions are based on the search for a more positive meaning for an experience than the one the person is currently creating.

I needed better answers to those questions than the one I'm used to hearing, which is "God never gives us more than we can handle." It is a well-intentioned sentiment, but it is actually very impractical and in my experience, sometimes quite harmful. If you're a fan of that advice that's fine, but at least allow me a moment to explain my position.

First of all, if you say something like "God never gives us more than we can handle" to a person who isn't handling it well, you've basically told them that they should be handling it and why aren't they. Not to mention you haven't given them any suggestions on how to handle it.

Please Visit www.LifeTeamStrategy.com

The main reason I believe this advice is impractical is because I've discovered time and time again how beneficial it is to be given more than you can handle. History is filled with the stories of people who when confronted with more than they could handle quickly grew into the person who could handle it. Why is that?

Because people don't become courageous, tenacious, strong, resilient, patient, compassionate or passionate unless they're put in situations that require it of them. As I said before, the human character is like a muscle; it only grows stronger with resistance. It doesn't grow stronger by only dealing with what it can handle—that only serves to keep it where it is.

Life routinely gives you more than you can handle in order to assist you in your evolution as a human being. Look around you: The nature of life is growth and creativity. If you were only given what you could handle, then nothing would ever require more of you than you're comfortable giving. Unless your comfort zone is penetrated there would never be a reason to adjust and expand it.

Based on everything I've discussed so far, I'd like to offer my alternative to "God never gives us any more than we can handle." I've concluded that the reason why adversity is flung so wholeheartedly in our lap at times is to enlist our participation in a universal personal development program I call "Angel Training." I'm not talking about angels in a religious sense; I'm referring to angels in the practical everyday sense. Have you ever said to someone "Oh, you're such an angel." Well, I have, and it has always been to a person who has helped me through a tough time and provided me with guidance that eased the suffering of the moment.

The greatest angels in life are the **Starters** who, when our lives are most chaotic, come along and not only support and encourage us but also GET IT. Why do they get it? Because they've been there. They went through it before us, and now they've come into our lives to show us the way.

The purpose of "Angel Training" is to actively necessitate our personal growth by giving us more than we can handle so we can become a person who can handle it. And in order to handle it, we must discover and implement the solution for overcoming it. Our graduation from "Angel Training" only occurs when we go out into the world, find people in similar circumstances and teach them the lessons we've learned. That, my friend, is what suffering is for. It is for your benefit—it is the universal conspiracy for your greatness and for equipping you to foster the greatness in others.

We begin our life education at the *School of Hard Knocks* and receive a full scholarship to the *University of Adversity*. If we learn our lessons well we go on to get a graduate degree called an *MBA*, or a *Masters of Beating Adversity*. If we get

Please Visit www.LifeTeamStrategy.com

really good at it we go even further toward our *Ph.D.*, which stands for *Doctor of Perpetual Hope*. When all is said and done we become the *CEO*, or *Creator of Extraordinary Outcomes*, where we take our place as the head of the greatest business of all—the business of living.

REMEMBERING BILL

I want to share with you the story of one of those special human beings who fully understood the meaning of Angel Training. His name was William Althouse. Although I never had the privilege of meeting him, I did have the great pleasure of getting to know about him through the memories of his daughter, Allison, who graciously allowed me to share a little piece of her late father with you. The following is a copy of the eulogy written and read by Allison's mother and Bill's widow, Barbara Althouse.

> *Some people go through life making mountains out of molehills. But not Bill—he did the impossible; he made molehills out of mountains. I think this was his most endearing trait. I know it was the one thing that attracted me to him over 25 years ago.*
>
> *The first time I saw Bill, he was slowly maneuvering down a long hallway. Even with the help of a walker, he was having great difficulty, and the look of concentration on his face was barely masking the pain he was feeling. I was astonished to hear that he was on his way to see the district manager in the office where I was working. He evidently was ready to return to work. I couldn't imagine why anyone in that condition would want to return to work so soon. Then, I learned, it really wasn't soon at all. Two and a half years had already passed from the day of his motorcycle accident. It was some time after when I heard the details of his injuries: two broken femurs, one completely shattered; a foot so damaged and disfigured it was almost amputated; a broken nose, arm and thumb; and a traumatic heart murmur.*
>
> *He had been through body casts, traction, numerous surgeries and bone grafts. After all was said and done, he was left with a leg two inches shorter than the other, a knee that wouldn't bend, a club foot, a hell of a limp, and arthritis. Pretty serious stuff, by most people's standards. Although he admitted at that time that it was the hardest thing he had ever faced, he never complained. Instead he joked about how it would have been tragic if he had broken his drinking arm.*
>
> *He joked about all the dates he could now get from the "concerned" ladies. He joked about how at the end of a long day at work when his limp was getting bad, he would see his friends walking toward him, and they didn't know it, but they were limping, too—what he called "feeling his pain." He was thankful that he hadn't lost his life or his limbs, and obviously considered his suffering minor in*

comparison to those he saw suffering around him. He felt the same way about his cancer, too.

He played it down and often consoled those who were calling to console him. Yes, Bill was very adept at making molehills out of mountains. If he was angry about his cancer, he didn't show it. In truth, I was angry enough for both of us. But after living with Bill all these years, I have learned a thing or two about acceptance and gratitude. Yes, he left us much too soon, but we were blessed that he even survived that accident 28 years ago. When he was diagnosed with pancreatic cancer, he was only given two to six months to live. He turned it into two and three-quarters years. He fought his cancer long and hard, with courage, determination, faith, hope, but most of all, with love. He loved us all. And it was that love that gave him the ability to do the impossible, make molehills out of mountains.

The following is taken from a card that Bill's daughter, Allison, sent out to those who knew and loved him.

My DAD

My Dad was liked by most people.
If you told him you liked the picture on the wall,
he'd pull it down and hand it to you.
He taught us how to give.

My Dad was a hard worker.
He went to work early and left late every day he could.
He took pride in his work and taught us to do the same.

My Dad cared about everyone.
He would limp in three feet of snow to help a stranger
change their flat tire. He taught us to care for all people.

My Dad is the best father anyone could have.
He always told us kids he loved us, and we all knew he
would do anything for Mom and us.
He taught us how to be a family.

My Dad was a great man.
He fought hard to live but left us too early.
I have learned so much from him, and his memory will live on forever.

Please Visit www.LifeTeamStrategy.com

Bill Althouse was an Angel on Earth in every sense of the word. He also understood what it meant to be a **Starter** in the lives of those around him. He thought of "we" before he thought of "I." He chose the kind of world he wanted to live in and then created that world for himself and those around him. This world is better because Bill was in it. And my life is better because of the impact he made on Allison, who has become a good friend to me. God Bless you, Bill, and thanks for the memories.

8

The ZAP

Next I want to talk to you about the extreme importance of being fully aware of the strength and flow of the emotional energy in your life. In particular, the flow of energy in your relationships is one of the primary determinants of whether you feel supported or thwarted and whether you grow or slow in life.

One of the best ways I've discovered to maintain and maximize your own emotional energy level is by understanding and utilizing the principle of osmosis. **Osmosis** refers to the process by which a substance of higher concentration in one area moves into an area of lower concentration until balance is achieved.

A simple way to explain this process is by imagining you had a cup with a hole in the side. Now imagine that you placed this cup in a pool of water a few inches deep. What will happen is the cup will fill with water through the hole in the side of it. It won't fill all the way to the top. It will only fill until the level of water inside the cup is even with the level of water outside the cup. When the levels are even, you've achieved balance. You've achieved it through a process called osmosis.

The same principle that works for the transfer of water between a pool and a cup, also works for the transfer of emotional energy between one person and another in a relationship. This occurs through a process I call **Emotional Osmosis.**

Think about a time you saw someone with a bad mood pass it on to others around him or her. Or think about how someone who is filled with joy is able to lift the spirits of someone who is sad, and you'll quickly realize what I'm talking about. Now let's talk about how you can use this principle to enhance the quality of your life by exploring a phenomenon called burnout.

I describe burnout as "a consuming feeling of physical and or emotional drain that leaves a person unable to give anymore of themselves." Burnout occurs as a direct result of giving and giving and giving out without getting back. In other words, you begin with a high concentration of energy and then give too much away. You go beyond giving in order to create balance, yet you actually "over-give" and leave yourself depleted, or burned out.

When you feel imbalance coming on, you need to stop and ask yourself, "When was the last time I had the opportunity to be given to?" Chances are it's been awhile, or the amount you took in was insufficient and now you're on the verge of burnout. The good news is that if you are depleted, the principle of Emotional Osmosis dictates that you will naturally be recharged with positive energy when exposed to a higher concentration than you currently possess.

Remember the cup? If the cup was empty and there was only a little bit of water outside it, then the cup would only be filled a little bit. The more depleted you are, the greater the source of positive emotional energy you will need to receive in order to recharge your emotional battery. This is where the composition of your Life Team is critical.

If you surround yourself with **Starters**, then they can be a fountain of youth in terms of positive energy. It is difficult to become burned out when surrounded by **Starters** because they give as much or more than they get. In many instances your cup will runneth over. Being surrounded by **Sneezers** can provide an additional boost of energy because of all the encouragement they give you.

You run into ripe territory for burnout when your Life Team is primarily represented by **Shovers** and **Shouters** who sap your energy with their negativity. When this happens, your Life Team is out of balance and it is time to implement the Z.A.P.

Implementing the ZAP

The ZAP stands for **Zero Asshole Policy** or **Zero Antagonist Policy** if you prefer. The rule of the ZAP is simple: If a relationship makes you better, then tap it; if it makes you worse, then ZAP it. I advise everyone to strip their Life Team down to the bones if necessary in order to rid themselves of the relationships that make them worse instead of better. I also encourage them to make the ZAP one of the only rules in life that is inflexible, right up there with the rule of looking both ways before crossing the street. Both rules, when adhered to, provide for your continued healthy existence.

Make sure the members of your Life Team know about this policy also. Just recently I was begged by a loved one to go to dinner with someone whom I knew would be **Shouting** negativity the whole time. Without hesitation I said, "Spending time with that person would be in direct violation of my Zero Asshole Policy." I didn't budge from my position, and neither should you. If somebody is

Please Visit www.LifeTeamStrategy.com

energetically detrimental to you, then they have lost the right to your time. How do you know when it's time to implement the ZAP?

To remain energized you have to be adamant about getting energy and locating the sources of energy available to you. I'd say that about 95% of our energy comes from our relationships. How can you determine whether a relationship offers more energy or drainage? As I said, when a relationship gives you more energy than it takes, and makes you better by being a part of it, that is the kind of relationship you want to embrace. This is the single most important determinant of whether a relationship is healthy or not. Are you better because of it?

So take an inventory of the relationships in your life. Are your relationships making you better or worse, are they helping you grow or slow? If they're helping you slow, then they have got to go—ZAP. You wouldn't keep eating food that was making you sick, would you?

Once you identify the relationships in your life that are making you better, determine what it is about them that makes you better? This is very important to know because when you can spot it you can get more of it and you can use it as a criterion when forming other relationships.

Now start thinking about how this criterion applies to your work environment. How does your work make you better? Which coworkers give you oxygen, and which ones put a bag over your head?

The next thing you need to gauge is the effect you have on others. Remember the universe works best in give-and-take relationships. So what kind of energy are you giving to others? Are you a **Starter** to some and a **Shouter** to others?

If a person has a higher concentration of negative energy than you have positive, which way is the Emotional Osmosis going to flow? In your direction, and it will sap your positive emotional energy. I see this all the time. ZAP that person if only for the moment so they don't infect you.

DEALING WITH NEGATIVE PEOPLE

Unfortunately there are situations where implementing the ZAP is more difficult. For example, in order to perform you job you may need to deal with coworkers you otherwise would have long ago given the ZAP. In these cases, the solution is to at least diffuse the effect they have on you. I've discovered two powerful strategies for handling these human speed bumps when they burst into your life.

The first strategy requires you to read between the lines and creatively assign meaning to the content of the words or actions of the person confronting you. It really doesn't matter who the person is. They may offer you destructive feedback or any variety of insult. Whether they're in a bad mood and looking to vent or are just looking to upset you is irrelevant. What matters is how you choose to interpret their efforts to make the most of the encounter. The idea is to demonstrate to this individual that their **Shoving** and **Shouting** negativity will not have a negative effect on a **Starter** like you.

A sure fire way to totally disarm their negativity is, after they're done sharing their thoughts with you, just look them in the eye and express complete "gratitude for their attitude." Remember you're looking for any opportunity to make this experience useful. So when they say things like "You're the most incompetent, useless person I know," look them in the face and sincerely say, "Thank you." As a **Starter**, you're deciding what you want to get from this encounter. So what are you thanking them for, you might ask. Their harsh words? No way. You're thanking them for the part of their statement that was of value to you—their honesty. You're also thanking them for taking the time out of their clearly busy schedule to share their feelings with you.

I'm not suggesting you do this to avoid dealing with feedback that you actually need to hear but might not be in the mood to listen to. This is to help you diffuse the effects of a verbal attack and to take the wind out of the sails of the attacker. Even if the attacker looks at you like you're nuts for the way you responded, the fact of the matter is, you have not been mentally or emotionally compromised by the attack. You could have easily become a **Shouter** and argued with them, but you're a **Starter**, and this approach allows you to remain so without compromising your standards.

The ZAP not only applies to people; it applies to your thoughts as well. In order to apply this policy consistently and effectively, you need to learn to pick and choose wisely what you're going to give your attention to. You need to determine what information is most important to you and most worthy of your attention. If you're in a pessimistic frame of mind, you're inclined to give 95% of your attention to the 5% of an event you don't like. With the **Starter** mindset, you're giving 100% of your attention to the content that is actually useful to you. Picking and choosing what we want to pay attention to isn't a new idea. We just need to be more deliberate and disciplined about it.

The second strategy I've discovered is to help prevent you from becoming infected by those **Shouters** who spend their lives either in crisis mode or focusing on the cloud instead of the silver lining. These are the people who, when you ask them the question "How are you?" respond with "How much time have you got?" They will then go into a lengthy, sometimes exhausting and detailed

Please Visit www.LifeTeamStrategy.com

description about everything that's wrong with their lives. When they've finished and anxiously await you to join them in their pity party, you respond according to the rules of the **Conspiracy of Positivity**. The basic rule in the conspiracy is that the universe is conspiring in your best interest—you need only to cooperate, another **Starter** concept. Negative people aren't cooperating—they're resisting the lessons of life which is why they're suffering. But since you understand the conspiracy you respond to their situation according to what you see.

When these people insist on focusing on the down side, you act as though what they're experiencing is the best thing that's ever happened to them. You respond enthusiastically with statements like, "That's great! Think of the opportunity you have to turn things around." You can also say, "Wow what a fantastic challenge. I can't wait to see what you do with this." I don't expect you to say these exact phrases, just understand that they are informed by solution-focused thinking when someone confronts you with their negative thinking.

One clarification needed here is that this approach isn't meant to be used with someone who has just experienced a traumatic event and is being negative as a result. Negativity in this case is usually a result of emotional shock and is understandable. This is for those folks who've made negativity a way of life.

Experience has taught me that for habitually negative people, the Conspiracy of Positivity is far more effective in turning their attitude around than statements like, "Look on the bright side," "You've got to think more positive," or "Awe don't talk like that, things will get better." These responses may sound like **Sneezing,** but in this context they're useless because they don't offer solutions. However, when you respond with an attitude that demonstrates enthusiasm for their situation as well as confidence in their ability to turn things around, it sounds less like a lecture or a pep talk and more like a sincere reaction. That's the kind of **Sneezing** you want to offer a person. True **Sneezing** offers encouragement based on the facts while saying something like, "Things will get better" with no way to back up the statement.

One of the down sides or benefits to this strategy depending on how you look at it is if the person in question is determined to remain negative and is more interested in pity than solutions (believe me they exist). What will likely happen in response to your attitude is that they will simply not come to you again and will instead look for someone else to dump on who will give them the pity they're looking for. They will have in essence ZAPPED themselves from your life. Either way, one thing is certain: You can change no one; the only thing you can do is master your own response and effectiveness in any given situation, which will in turn offer them an opportunity to change theirs.

Please Visit www.LifeTeamStrategy.com

Your Life Team Directory

Sometimes before implementing the ZAP, it's helpful to compile a list of everyone on your life team as well as the role they currently play in your life. You can make this list in a diary, a personal organizer, address book or anywhere else you make lists. The main difference is that in addition to their contact information you'll be noting their contribution to your life using the following terms: Starter, Sitter, Sneezer, Shover and Shouter.

The purpose, of course, is for you to be able to think more clearly about the quality of the people you surround yourself with. Identify all of the resources you have in your life, including friends, relatives, service people, businesses and anything else you have available to help you accomplish everything you want to. Think of this as your *personal resource inventory*. If there is a resource you need that you don't have, it will be noticeably absent from your list; therefore, you know you need to find it.

You can take this list as far as you want and include books or magazines you read as well as television programming that you watch. The more you monitor the actual contribution made by whatever you take in through your senses the more you can refine your life to include primarily those things that bring out the very best in you.

With each entry, explain what kind of a resource that person or business is. Next to one friend's name you might note first that they are a **Starter** and then provide details (I can call them any time of day or night, no matter what). Another friend might be noted as a **Shouter** (always complaining about things.) This kind of notation can be an efficient way of letting you know that it's time to edit your address book as well as your life.

I've found this to be a wonderful tool for reminding myself who means the most to me and why. It also reminds me to regularly acknowledge the **Starters** and **Sneezers** for their importance in my life. Once you understand each term of the Life Team Strategy^{TM} well enough, this simple designation makes it easier to flip through your address book and find just the right person for you at that moment.

Don't forget the first listing in your directory needs to be yourself. Although we need others in our lives to help us and offer us support, far too often we run to others for things we are perfectly capable of giving to ourselves. List your name first so that you start with yourself in any situation. List everything about yourself that is a resource—any abilities you have that you can rely on. Only after you've exhausted your own inherent resources do you turn to someone else on the list.

Please Visit www.LifeTeamStrategy.com

Selling yourself short or counting yourself out is one of the worst things you can do to yourself.

Your Life Team Diary

If you're having difficulty determining the kind of people in your life then there's one simple exercise you can do to help you find out. I recommend that you track the presence of Starters, Sitters, Sneezers, Shovers and Shouters in your life for one whole day. Write down who they are and what they do or say. For those of you who come home exhausted every day and don't know why, you might be shocked at how often the energy is being sucked out of you each day. After making this determination you can better determine who to stick with and who to ZAP.

Please Visit www.LifeTeamStrategy.com

9

Becoming the Ultimate Starter

Let's say you wake up in the morning and you want to plan the kind of day you're going to have. When you sit down to plan your day, where is the most logical place to begin? That's right at the end. By determining the end you desire, you can then determine the strategy you'll need to use to prepare yourself to achieve that end. The kind of strategy you will use in this case is called your **Preparation Strategy**.

Any result you plan to create is only as good as your preparation strategy, and part of that strategy is your meaning. The best way to determine where to start anything is to first determine where you want to end up. That's why you begin at the end.

For example, you can only prepare for a vacation when you know where you want to go. By preparing for each day with your end in sight you can then choose which preparation strategy you want to use to guide you. That is the ideal. Now let's look at the various things people do to prepare for their day.

What typically occurs in our lives is that something happens to us and then we try to assign meaning to it, after the fact. This meaning is usually a result of subconscious conditioning that we aren't really aware of. And because we aren't consciously involved in it I refer to this conditioning as a "re-action strategy" because it has more to do with habit than conscious, deliberate choice.

What I propose is a replacement for your "re-action" to life's events with deliberate "pro-action," which means you need an effective meaning strategy to inform your experience before you even have it. You need a "Preparation Strategy."

Believe it or not you can actually decide in advance what things are going to mean to you. In fact, you probably do it already. When you can do this you have complete power over your experience. Keep in mind I didn't say you control the events of your life—just your experience of them.

But before you choose the "Preparation Strategy" you want to use, you need to know and understand the one you're currently using. To determine this, ask and answer the following question: "How are you?" That's it. "How are you?" I recommend that you ask yourself that question the moment you open your eyes in the morning as well as periodically throughout the day. I wouldn't suggest walking around asking this question out loud, however. When you do that everyone around you will be able to answer that question for you and the answer might involve a straight jacket!

This question is profoundly valuable because the way you answer it determines which "Preparation Strategy" you're using at that moment. Now let's see what your answer reveals. I have determined that there are generally four main answers to the question "How are you?" that are the basis of the **Four Preparation Strategies**.

The four main answers are…

a. Not good

b. Fine

c. Great

d. And the fourth I'll get to in a moment

First allow me to use a metaphor to explain the Four Preparation Strategies. Imagine you are looking out into the horizon and you see half of the sun sitting above the horizon and half of the sun is sitting below. The strategy you use determines the meaning you assign to what you're seeing in this case.

For example:

The **Pessimist** sees a **sunset**.

The **Optimist** sees a **sunrise**.

The **Realist** sees the sun half up half down.

The fourth response is that of the **Realistic Optimist** who says that sunset or sunrise, all that matters is where opportunity lies.

The **Pessimist** tends to see it **worse than it is.**

Please Visit www.LifeTeamStrategy.com

The **Optimist** tends to see it **better than it is.**

The **Realist** sees it **as it is.**

But the **Realistic Optimist** sees how it is as well as the potential it has. Unlike the other three mindsets, the **Realistic Optimist** is first and foremost action-oriented—always on the look out for how to improve a situation. This is the mindset of the **Starter**. Now let's look at each strategy individually by examining how each one answers the question "How Are You?" first thing in the morning.

The **Pessimist** says, "Why did I even get out of bed?"

The **Optimist** says, "Nothing but blue skies ahead."

The **Realist** says, "Whatever happens happens."

The **Realistic Optimist** says, "No matter what happens I will use it as an opportunity to become better."

Based on the Four Preparation Strategies, which one do you feel will produce a day of experiences with more useful meaning than the others? Why is that? The Preparation Strategy you use determines what opportunities you will spot in the course of your day. Clearly there are other opportunities available to you; you just don't see them because you're not looking for them.

UNLIMITED HOPE

I've found that there is a key component of the Realistic-Optimist Preparation Strategy that really makes it work. That key in the human mind seems able to turn the saddest person into the gladdest person, and is capable of generating strength in a single person or an entire nation.

That one key factor is **Hope**. Hope is one of the most powerful motivators there is. It has helped people survive being wrongfully imprisoned; it helped people survive wars and captivity in Nazi concentration camps.

Hope can make anything survivable or at least endurable. I've found through my life that those who've been able to find hope in any situation were those who had two things at their disposal: the knowledge of their options and an ability to create positive meaning for their experiences. With that in mind, let's define hope as **"the experience of empowerment derived from the knowledge of your options."**

Having the knowledge of your options helps you realize that situations have many exits that only need to be found. Those who are hopeless see no way out and believe that they are stuck or totally screwed. Those who are hopeless also choose to decide to see challenges negatively, as punishment. Such an attitude can paralyze a person with fear and self-pity.

A person without hope is a person who has embraced a negative way of assigning meaning to their life. It is meaning that helps fuel hope; there is no hope without a strong sense of meaning. Think again about your career choice. Why that career and not something else? Why have you chosen to do what you do?

Do you do what you do because you feel there are no other options available to you, or do you do it because you assign more meaning to doing that as opposed to something else? The fact of the matter is that the more options you discover the more solutions you will uncover and the more hope you have that a solution will be found.

I stumbled upon a wonderful technique for generating options while I was lying in my hospital bed during chemotherapy. Spending day after day staring at blank walls in a hospital can get pretty long and tiring, and the mind has a wonderful way of entertaining itself.

What I found myself doing was looking at each object in the room and thinking of ways to use it for other than it's intended purpose. I found myself seeing the clock on the wall as a hat, a Frisbee, a plate, or the top of a stool.

I looked at a pencil and saw a spear, half of a pair of chop sticks, something to prop up the window with or pick my nose with (just an example, not a recommendation).

What I found was that I was training my brain to look beyond the obvious and instead at the potential of a situation. You will be amazed at the number and quality of options that you generate and the amount of hope that you create.

BEING RIGHT OR BEING HAPPY

One way a person can stand in the way of a life filled with hope is in wanting to be right all the time. Because as people we like to be right, we generally look for evidence that we are right. If we begin the day with a strong Pessimistic Preparation Strategy what are we looking for? Evidence to support that we're right to think pessimistically. The rule is "You can be right or you can be happy, but you can't be both."

Because people who are committed to being right all the time are investing their minds in inflexibility. There are people who have fought tooth and nail to avoid change from happening. But I'll let you in on a little secret. I've never met anyone who died of a little change.

Being right is more or less impossible to do because being right is totally in the moment. What is right is often right for a given set of circumstances. Once the circumstances change, what is right for them could change as well. So I am in no way telling you that the information I'm providing is right for you. That's your decision. What I can help you do is to generate options and solutions to help you move your life in directions that will hopefully lift yourself to higher points in your life.

Because as I said, life isn't about being right, it's about being productive and about being effective. It's about having a life filled with a meaning that compels you to act in such a way that your every thought and action generates quality in your life and in the lives of those around you.

This attitude of always being on the lookout for ways to improve or extract the greatest amount of quality from all of life's circumstances is what the Realistic Optimistic Preparation Strategy is all about? If you adopt this strategy then you're looking for opportunities to learn and grow no matter what happens.

THE RIGHT THING TO DO

There is a big difference between "Being Right" and "Doing Right." The biggest difference is in who benefits in the outcome. "Being Right" is all about you, your ego and the satisfaction of being right. It is a very selfish, competitive and one-sided position to take. People who want to be right all the time are **Shovers** competing for superiority in an argument and often finding themselves alone a lot because they put their needs in a relationship first.

"Doing Right" is the **Starter** perspective and is less about "you" and more about "us." It considers the needs of the situation as superior to the needs of your individual ego. "Doing right" is the "service mindset." You know that you're doing the right thing if it is done in service to others. Whenever I meet someone new I ask myself, "How can I be of service to this person?" Immediately I'm thinking about how to be a **Starter** for this person and how to make knowing me worthwhile. I think of ways to bring value to this person's life.

Please Visit www.LifeTeamStrategy.com

Now, let's take this a step further and think beyond meeting each new person in this manner and extend this mindset to meeting each new day in this way. Why not begin each new day by asking yourself, "How can I be of service today?" "How can I bring value to this day?" "How can I make sure that my life will make today better somehow?" This is a solid Realistic Optimistic Preparation Strategy, and it is very difficult to be self-centered with this mindset.

Assume this approach for only one day and see how much more deliberately you live your life that day. More important, see the difference in your relationships when you suddenly focus on how to bring value to them each and everyday. Prepare to be astounded.

Two Goals for Everyday Growth

When I wake up each morning, I do so with the absolute resolve to accomplish two very important goals by the day's end. I've chosen these two particular goals for the simple fact that by accomplishing them, I'm guaranteed to experience an increase in the quality of my day and will likely increase the quality of someone else's day as any **Starter** would. These two goals are to simply:

1. Learn something
2. Teach something

Pretty simple, huh? Why these two goals do you ask? Because their sole purpose is to ensure that I grow somehow each and every day and help someone else to do the same. This guarantees that life will always give me something new and will never be boring. You'd be surprised just how easy it is to accomplish each goal. For example, you can accomplish Goal #1 simply by reading a few pages in a book. I'm talking about a book that provides you information that you didn't have before, that stirs your mind, invigorates your spirit, and, most important, provides information you can use, take action on and actually apply in your life the moment you've read it. I'm not talking about reading something that serves only as distraction.

When achieved at every opportunity, Goal #1 will produce a guaranteed result each time. You'll find that when someone asks you the question, "What's New?" you will never, ever be compelled to answer by saying, "Nothing." A life filled with quality is a life filled with newness. When you improve yourself, you keep things new, vibrant and growing. That's just one suggestion; there are countless ways to accomplish this goal.

Please Visit www.LifeTeamStrategy.com

Goal #2 is a piece of cake. The easiest way to accomplish this goal begins by asking one simple question to someone else: "How are you?" It sounds cliché, and we probably ask this question 100 times a day. The difference here is that the answer you're given determines your course of action. If the answer to the question is in the negative, then all you have to do is provide the person in question with the opportunity to improve themselves in that moment. For example, I do the grocery shopping for my family and am always exposed to very tired and often grumpy cashiers. So when I ask the question, "How are you?" it can be answered in the negative via their statements or their body language. I, of course, reply to their answer by telling him or her what a wonderful job they're doing and how much I appreciate how quickly they help me get in and out. I then thank them by name and encourage them to ask for a raise. They inevitably are standing a little taller with a big smile on their face as I walk out.

Another way to help someone else improve themselves is simply by catching a person in the act of doing something right. There is nothing more empowering than subtly encouraging people to be on the look out for evidence of their own competence. If you're always spotting it then they begin to look for it themselves, and before long their mind shifts in favor of the positive. Of course, it isn't your job or my job to change someone else's mind. But you can offer them the opportunity.

What matters is that Goals #1 and #2 are pursued and achieved with the utmost enthusiasm and sincerity. So when someone asks you the question, "How are you?" you can truthfully answer, "Better than yesterday, and getting better all the time!"

The best way to accomplish Goals #1 and #2 simultaneously is by becoming a mentor—a mentor for a moment, for a mile or for a good long while. We can't help but grow when we guide others to greatness. Think of mentoring as a form of person-to-person osmosis. When you share some of yourself with those you love just by being near them and giving only the very best of yourself, then you've done it all.

Happy "Cure Day!"

When is your Cure Day? Don't have one yet? Well, after reading this I'm positive you'll start having one. The very first Cure Day in my life occurred on September 26th, 1988—the day I was told I was in remission from cancer. That's the day that I was physically, spiritually and emotionally reborn. Although five years is commonly accepted as the minimum required survival period before someone is considered officially cured, I didn't wait. I started that day; I started everything over in my life. It was also the day I firmly took my life in my own hands with the unwavering commitment to do everything I could do to find solutions to my own suffering as well as the suffering of others, which it turns out are not so different.

September 26th is a day each and every year that I refer to as my official Cure Day. On that day I celebrate all of the people, places and things that had made my life better that year by being a part of it, because had I died from the cancer I wouldn't have had any of it. Now after all these years, my official Cure Day has become the day for the party, be it a dinner out or a cookout, during which I celebrate the new **Starters** and **Sneezers** in my life as well as those who've been in my life for previous Cure Days and continue to contribute to it. Sure, I thank them and show appreciation every day, but on this day I make stars of them, and I highly recommend you do the same for the **Starters** in your life. Cure Day has become something of a reverse birthday. It's a celebration of my rebirth, but instead of celebrating myself, I celebrate all of those who make it worthwhile.

I say that Cure Day is the party day because it wasn't long before I realized that I didn't want to wait an entire year to express the gratitude I feel every day for those who continue to make my life so glorious. So now Cure Day is a daily event, because every day I am exposed to people, places and experiences that allow me to get through the day and make myself a little better because I encountered them—thus curing me of my former self by helping me grow in some small or even gigantic way. Sometimes all a person does is comfort me with a kind word. In doing so they have helped cure me if even for a moment. It is this that I now celebrate.

In your daily life, everything within yourself that you've fixed, replaced or improved upon in anyway has cured you in some way. I'm not suggesting that you were previously in a diseased state. I'm using the word "cure" here to denote that a healing or the filling of a need or emptiness has taken place that allowed you to move forward.

So celebrate what's new about today, the people and the experiences. What's new about your future outlook because of new options you have discovered? Celebrate everything that's inspired you today. Cure Day is a celebration of everything that has come to you simply because you were given the privilege of living this day with all of the opportunities it provided for you.

Please Visit www.LifeTeamStrategy.com

Most important, make sure you take the time to celebrate yourself for being the kind of person who attracts the quality of people that you have in your life because of who you are. Happy Cure Day!

Final Thoughts

Well, if I've done my job correctly, then this has been one heck of a ride for you. I could easily write another 100 pages or so on shoring up your Life Team, adding more meaning to your life or how to become a better **Starter**. But what matters the most is that you now have some exceptional tools that you may not have had before to help you on your way.

This book doesn't contain everything you need for a balanced life; no book could do that, no matter what the marketing tells you. I've given you thoughts, observations, strategies and most of all opportunities. Opportunities to finally begin to put the pieces of your life in exactly the right places they need to be in order for you to get the kind of support and the kind of results you so richly deserve. I've done my part. The rest is up to you.

I want to finish this book with one final thought on the power of meaning. The main reason I am sitting here and am able to write this book for you is because I've been given a second chance at life. You have a second chance right now in this moment, a second chance at creating a life with all of the meaning you want. With the completion of every single breath, you begin and end a second chance at life.

A wise man was once asked the question, "How long is life?" His answer, "One breath." We enter this world with our first breath and exit this world with our last. With each breath our life starts over; it gives us a second chance. Now as you enter the next moment, your next life, you have nothing but opportunities.

So I end with this question "How are you?" Your answer to this question is the beginning of your second chance. Now that you have it, what are going to do with it?

Please Visit www.LifeTeamStrategy.com

Bibliography

Canfield, Jack (2000). The Self-Esteem and Peak Performance Facilitating Skills Seminar. From the workbook that accompanied this seminar (July 8–15, 2000), Santa Barbara, CA. For more information on this seminar visit www.jackcanfield.com

    Jack Canfield
    Self-Esteem Seminars, Inc.
    P.O. Box 30880
    Santa Barbara, CA 93103
    800-237-8336

Mary Beth Curran, Editor
mbdcurran@hotmail.com

Mary Beth edited this book and in my estimation helped me create a book that is ten times better than it would have been without her contribution. She is gifted at what she does and helped make my gift of writing even better. If you ever need a project of yours edited I can think of no one better to recommend for the job.

About the Author

Brian R. King is a Licensed Clinical Social Worker and Cancer Survivor. He is also the President of Change Your Life, Inc., which specializes in developing and teaching life-transformation techniques to help his clients to "Heal the Mind, Body and Spirit Through Simplicity." Brian is also known for his inspirational interactive speaking style, which has been called "a cross between Dr. Wayne Dyer and Bugs Bunny." You can find Brian online at www.LifeTeamStrategy.com

0-595-33332-X

Printed in the United States
130209LV00003B/205/A